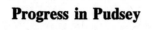

Progress in Pudsey

PROGRESS IN PUDSEY

Joseph Lawson

CALIBAN BOOKS

This edition first published 1978
by CALIBAN BOOKS
13 The Dock, Firle, Sussex BN8 6NY

ISBN 0904573079

Typeset in 8 on 11pt Ionic by
Eager Typesetting Company, 22a Westbourne Place, Hove, Sussex
and printed by
Newhaven Press, 44 Meeching Road, Newhaven, Sussex

Little is known about the life of Joseph Lawson, but the following brief biography was published in Charles Forshaw's *Yorkshire Poets Past and Present,* Volume I (1888):

"Born October 17th, 1821, at Pudsey, and author of a work lately published on 'Progress in Pudsey during the last sixty years,' which has received the unanimous praise of the newspaper press, as giving a 'true and vivid account of village life sixty years ago,' etc . . . Mr Lawson has been a great reader of our principal authors, besides newspaper literature, throughout his life, and contributed a large number of articles in prose on social, political, and other subjects, and also in verse, which have appeared during the last forty years in English and American newspapers and journals. In 1847 he took his wife and family to the United States of America, but after being there about two years he returned to this country on account of his wife's bad health. For nearly forty years he was a woollen manufacturer and merchant in England and America, but had to give up business some time ago on account of declining health, but has been fully occupied since in writing articles, etc, for the press . . . Mr Lawson has recently removed to Leeds."

This edition has been reset and reprinted from the 1887 original

LETTERS

TO THE YOUNG

ON

PROGRESS IN PUDSEY

DURING THE

LAST SIXTY YEARS

BY

JOSEPH LAWSON

Stanningley:

J. W. BIRDSALL, YORKSHIRE PRINTING AND PUBLISHING WORKS

—

1887

— Dedicated —

TO THE

PEOPLE OF PUDSEY

ESPECIALLY

THE YOUNG,

AT HOME AND ELSEWHERE

BY THEIR

WELL-WISHER AND FELLOW-TOWNSMAN,

THE AUTHOR

HORSFORTH,
March, 1887

PREFACE

In compliance with numerous requests, the following letters are issued in a separate form. Being written chiefly for the young people, who, from the nature of their position, cannot be expected to have large pecuniary resources at command, not having had a sufficient length of time to acquire much wealth, we have resolved to publish a cheap edition.

Our desire is that they should be read; thinking from our own experience, that the young people might be helped both to appreciate the superior advantages they possess as compared with their forefathers, and be prompted to greater activity on behalf of progress in the future.

The following letters extended over twice the length of time that we expected they would do when we began to write them, though we curtailed them as much as possible, compatible with giving the reader something like a general view of the various matters dealt with.

We are not conscious of having gone out of our way to deal with debatable matters, but have tried to avoid them as much as possible. One thing however is certain, that those who only read their own side deny themselves of some advantage which reading both sides would give. Were there no difference of opinion amongst mankind, no one could learn anything from his fellow-men, and all social intercourse and progress would be at an end.

There is no need for any apology on our part for the order or arrangement of our subject. The various letters were written as the matter presented itself and impressed us at the time, and it has not been deemed desirable to alter them in that respect, though some slight alterations and corrections have been made.

It is only necessary to add that if any person 50 years ago had predicted what has since come to pass, he would have been considered crazy. And could anyone foresee, and tell us the social, political, and religious aspects of Pudsey 50 years hence, he also would probably be thought a fit subject for Bedlam. Change and progress seem so slow from day to day, that it is only by looking back over a long period of time that we are able to see the immense progress made. We trust that to some extent the following letters will enable the reader to do this.

THE AUTHOR

Horsforth, Sept. 8th, 1886

CONTENTS
CHAPTER I
The Old Time Roads, Buildings, Furniture, etc.

CHAPTER II
Scarcity of Coal, Light, Soap, Water, etc.

CHAPTER III
Baking, Brewing, Dress, Food, etc.

CHAPTER IV
Courtship and Love-Making

CHAPTER V
Old Time Weddings

CHAPTER VI
What is the Chief Employment?

CHAPTER VII
The Trials and Difficulties of Hand-Loom Weavers

CHAPTER VIII
Burling and Burlers

CHAPTER IX
Low State of Education

CHAPTER X
"Superstition the Child of Ignorance"

CHAPTER XI
Manners, Customs, Sports and Pastimes

CHAPTER XII
Theological Progress

CHAPTER XIII
Contributory Causes of Change and Progress in the Manufacture of Woollens

CHAPTER XIV
Power Looms, and the Revolution they Effected

CHAPTER XV
Fulneck

CHAPTER XVI
Tong

CHAPTER XVII
Progress in Music

CHAPTER XVIII
The Hall of Freedom Project

CHAPTER XIX
Progress in the Future

CHAPTER XX
Concluding Chapter

LETTERS
TO THE YOUNG
ON
PROGRESS IN PUDSEY
DURING THE LAST SIXTY YEARS

CHAPTER I

The Old Time Roads, Buildings, Furniture, etc.

Pudsey at present the centre of a Parliamentary Division—Its general condition 60 years ago—No order or taste in the buildings—A view of the roads and side walks—Surface drains—Ash-middens and filth—Scanty conveniences—A peep into a house—A doctor's first medicine—Ovens—Sanded stone floors—The oaken "Kist"—Corner cupboard—Delfcase—Mutual help—Borrowing and lending.

Since Pudsey, by the late Reform Bills, has been made the Centre of a Parliamentary Division, and elected its first Member to represent it in the British House of Parliament, an old native is led to ponder on times far back in the past, and compare such with the present.

Pudsey may not have made that *rapid* progress which some other places have done, owing to their more favoured situation, or other special advantages, yet, if some old inhabitant who had left the village 60 years ago, and never seen or heard of it since, could revisit it today, he would be a sort of second Rip Van Winkle. Or could the young men, who are natives of Pudsey, be placed in the village at the period referred to, and be compelled to make their way in it for twelve months, they would be severely puzzled. The appearance of the buildings, roads, and inhabitants; the homes, food, and dress; the native habits and customs; employment, sports, and pastimes; bad situations, and *unavoidable dense ignorance;* were such, though in all respects equal to the surrounding villages at that time, as no one who has not lived amongst it can fully realise, for words in such matters convey but a faint idea of the actual state of things. Yet, during all that period, progress for the time being always seemed slow and almost imperceptible, and it is only by carrying the mind back for many years, and comparing the past with the present, that we are able to see the immense changes and improvements that have taken place.

At that time there would only be about one-third of the present population, and the houses in most parts were *scattered*. There were no Local Boards, and persons built houses to suit their own personal *whim* or interest, regardless of taste, order, or sanitary considerations; hence they appeared as if they had sprung up from seeds dropped unawares, to be *weeded* out by coming generations, placed here and there as if by accident, approached by crooked *folds,* or courts, and narrow passages called *ginnels,* etc., though a stranger had less difficulty in finding a person than might be supposed, as everyone knew nearly all the rest of the people.

Let us, in our imagination, view the roads, etc., in those days. Many of them we find with irregular gradients, up hill and down hill, to the discomfort of man and beast. Other parts have narrow and dangerous places, and in wet weather, especially during a *thaw,* the highways are almost impassible, and particularly so are those streets or lanes leading off from the main roads. Then the sidewalks, or *causeways:* we find some of them un-flagged, and such as are have only a single flagstone in width; in many parts much higher than the streets. They are very dangerous, especially on dark nights and in frost and snow, with unlighted streets; but to obviate the difficulty somewhat, many are carrying lanterns in their hands, with a candle inside, to see their way and avoid a *collision.* This reminds us of the complaints made by some at the present day of the tendency to Socialism there is in our legislation. Now lighting the streets with gas is *socialistic,* but few will deny that it has a great advantage over the old lantern system, which left everyone at his own option, whether he provided for himself that sorry flicker of a light, or walked and plodded his way on dangerous roads in midnight darkness. Whatever good can be done better by *united action* than by *isolated* individual effort is a public benefit.

But let us pursue our course of inspection, and we see on the surface slops and other refuse which have come from the dwellings, and heaps of ashmiddens, and other filth, exposed to the gaze of every passer by. Many of the houses have no outside conveniences, and the occupants are at the mercy of those who have; whilst many of those owned by others are in a most repulsive condition, for, as we have said, there is no Local Board to correct the nuisance.

Let us peep into the people's dwellings: we find the rooms very low, and windows small, for glass is dear. The houses, being either badly drained, or not drained at all, are mostly damp. There are few sashes in the windows, and seldom an air-pane for ventilation. There is dense ignorance of sanitary science. A doctor comes into a house where there is fever, and he knocks a pane of glass out with his stick, his first dose of medicine being fresh air.

Many of the houses have no ovens, and the occupants have to bake on a "bakstone" placed on the fire, or carry their dough to a neighbour who has an oven, taking coal to heat it. Few have iron castings for the fireplace, but large stones instead, which they make black with blacklead or with what they call *"oil of coil"*. These stones often break with the heat of the fire, and have to be replaced. Such as have iron castings, ovens, etc., have to put them in themselves as tenants, and risk getting a valuation when they leave the house. They have mostly stone floors, which they wash and sprinkle with sand, which they "bray" or crush from stones they buy from shops and carts, or get them from the roads, walls, or quarries, and some scour the hearth stone and doorsteps with scouring stone. Most of the working people's houses are meagrely furnished; many have no clock or timepiece, and may be seen going frequently during the day to where there is one, to know the time. In some houses there is an oaken *Chest* or *Kist*—a family *heirloom*, or a small cupboard fastened up in a corner, and a *delfcase* for pots and plates; but pots are dear, and much of a coarse kind of ware is used, such as brown and black.

It is pleasing, in these rude times, to see the mutual good-will and friendship there is, notwithstanding the occasional *back-biting, tittle-tattle,* and *ill-will.* They watch and nurse each other's families when sick, and borrow and lend almost anything in the house; though I am not aware that they equal the folks in a neighbouring village, where it is said they borrow *basins of broth* and *pots and plates of porridge.*

CHAPTER II

Scarcity of Coal, Light, Soap, Water, etc.

Few cellars and coalhouses—"Muleloads of Coal", and the coal heap—Raking the fire—and lighting it—Candles—The fire-side on a winter's night—Soap and its substitutes—Pumping, drawing, and fetching water—Waiting till it springs—Cellar wells and ponds—Panic on a washing day—Catching the eavedrops.

Many families have no cellars or outbuildings to put their coal in, and have to leave it outside. When a deep snow falls, they have much shovelling to find their piles. It frequently happens that some neighbour whose coal "heap" or pile is either used up, or getting low, helps himself or herself from others which are often in close proximity. This is not mere jealousy or suspicion, because the coal had been put in a definite form to be sworn to, on a certain night, and on the following morning the pile was found to be disarranged, and remarkably less in bulk. Few persons can afford to keep much coal by them, and many fetch from retailers a hundredweight at a time in a wheelbarrow. Others buy a bag from off the top of cartloads, while many order what they call a "Muleload", which is a sackful fetched on a donkey's back. There are persons who keep a drove of these donkeys, which they drive daily down Scholebrook Lane to the Tong side of the *Beck* to Holme and other places for coals. It would touch the feelings of any right-minded person to see the animals struggling under their loads up the steep hills. Some have their backs in a most horrible state from wounds made by the coal, whilst others have sores on their legs, caused by the bites of dogs kept to drive them along. Then it is quite common to see the poor animals fall down under their load, and in wet weather the roads are such that their feet stick in the clay and mud, so that stumbling and tumbling is a constant occurrence. Those who get a cartload of coal at a time seldom know what weight they get. Some of the "coal-leaders", as they are called, have carts made small to make a little load appear a big one. Others have bags of coal on the top, which they sell to customers on the road, and, it is said, do not deduct them where they deliver the rest, though all are weighed together at the pit. Some bring cartloads of coal from Bierley and Dudley

Hill, and hawk them from door to door, and the purchasers are not always the poorest of the inhabitants; many persons who are known to be in good circumstances buy their coal in these various ways.

Lighting the fire is no easy matter, for there are no Lucifer Matches; hence those who can afford the fuel, use means to prevent it going out. They "rake" the fire, as it is called, by covering it at bed-time with small coal and cinders, and make it compact, so that it may burn till morning. When it is not kept in, there is serious trouble sometimes in lighting it. If the chimney does not draw well, at an outside place away from other dwellings, much time is wasted; for, after striking fire from flint, etc., so as to light paper and a candle, persons may be seen blowing with their mouths or fanning with a board to light the chips, till their eyes are red and full of tears caused by the smoke being puffed back in their faces. Those living near each other, light their candle at some of their neighbours' fires, or borrow a little fire, or exchange a piece of coal for some, except at Christmas time when it is thought unlucky to do so. Yes: raking a fire and lighting one are serious matters; and, as in everything else so it is in these two, persons vary very much in their ability to do them scientifically. Then, candles are dear, and melt and waste much, especially if carried about the house. Many families make it a rule never to light one except for some work that cannot be done without, and then it is immediately blown or snuffed out.

If one goes into a neighbour's house (as some, it is said, do on a winter's night on purpose to save their own fire and candles), he will probably find a few sitting round the fire, and he is mostly some time ere he is able to recognise all those present, for seldom is there any light, except from the fire, which cannot at all times give out much light, and there is some truth in the remark that during the winter season people do not see each other clearly. There may be some use in this darkness after all, for soap is at a high price, and some slight defects in one's personal appearance for want of its freer use may not be so prominent. Soap, we say, is dear, and many substitutes are resorted to by some families; at times a little oatmeal, etc., and something else we will not mention as well, except that it bears some not distant relationship to what is collected in barrel-carts to scour cloth with at the mills.

But the most lamentable affair in our estimation in relation to cleanliness and health, is the condition of Pudsey, at the time we are speaking of, as regards its water supply, or rather the want of it; not that it is worse off than other villages with its population are. During a wet season there is plenty, such as it is but in many cases it is too far to fetch. Some few have pumps, but too often out of repair. One here and there who has a cellar may have a well in it, probably in a house undrained, or badly drained, except so far as their cellar well may do it. There are a few draw-wells where the "Iron-bound bucket" is often lost, and the well has to be dredged with "well-creepers", while a dozen persons may be waiting for water. There are ponds in the village for cattle, but the water is not all that is desirable, being a little spoiled by the rotting carcases of dogs and cats, though it is said some publicans use it for brewing. There are public wells in every part of the village, but during a dry season it is a terrible affair getting water, for most of the wells are dry, and remind one of the African desert. The washing days produce a panic. Scores of people spend half their time in fetching water, for many have to go more than half a mile for it, and have sore heads and blistered hands with kits and cans. Sometimes may be seen 20 or 30 vessels waiting by the side of the well to take their turn as the water springs, and strong conscienceless men and women cheat the weaker out of their turns. The water carried so far, too, is often muddy, and has to stand to let the sediment settle before being used; and how people manage to live and maintain even moderate health is a mystery, but nature must have a deal of elasticity in her to bear such stress and violation of her laws. During rain scores of bowls, tubs, etc., may be seen under the eaves catching the droppings to wash the clothes! There are few spouts, so that one is soon wet through in passing under the eave-drops on entering a house.

What we have said about the difficulties of procuring water sixty years ago in Pudsey comes far short of conveying a full idea of the sad state of things then existing. Both brewing and washing days were frequently put off for the want of water, while, on the other hand, if no rain had fallen for some time, people would wash their clothes before the regular time, lest the springs should fail; or if a good shower of rain came, they would rush out and put their tubs and bowls, etc., under the eave-drops to catch them, and would wash a day or two sooner, whilst the water caught was sweet and fresh.

CHAPTER III

Baking, Brewing, Dress, Food, etc.

Planning for Washing—Brewing beer called "drink"—Food—
Flour dear, and why—Flesh meat a luxury—"Havver cake" and
the "Bakstone"—Borrowing and lending yeast—Brewing utensils
—Drink in every house—All welcome to "a sup o' drink"—The
parson and cobbler drink it—Thought to possess more strength
than any other article.

There is not very much to say about people's dress at this
time. It is mostly made of plain home-spun material, and any
observer will soon find that fashions and styles last a long time.
Many of the women have bed-gown dresses, and bib dresses,
white caps, made of muslin, linen or cambric. The screeds are
largely fluted with what they call a *"tallying iron"* (probably
meaning *Italian* iron), after being washed and starched. These
caps look neat when "well got up", as they call it, and some
women pride themselves in being able to get up their caps
nicely. The old women, or many of them, tie a black ribbon
round their heads, to keep up their hair and for ornamentation,
and under which they stick their knitting needles. Bonnets are
plainly made, having pasteboard foundations shaped by the
milliners from paper patterns. Eighteen pence is about the average price charged for making a dress or a bonnet. The women,
except on a Sunday, seldom wear a bonnet, but throw over their
heads a kerchief or shawl. The men have mostly a thick
spun material, with very little finish, if any, and in many cases
buckskin breeches which button or tie at the knee, and the stock-
ings all exposed, except that some of the richer sort have gaiters
or leggings, and buckled shoes. They seldom get new suits—very
few in a life-time, but the material is sound and strong, being
made of pure wool, mungo and shoddy being unknown. They
have black down hats with broad brims that they call beavers,
which are made to do service for many years, and some wear
the same hat most of their lifetime. Both women and men wear
straight shoes (not lefts and rights), and when worn on one side
a little, the right foot shoe is changed for the left, and worn
straight or even again. During the working days, many of the
men wear blue linen smocks and aprons, but some have what

looks nicer, wolsey aprons, striped blue, or black and white. A silk dress is seldom seen; but for a wedding dress, or for special occasions, a few have dresses made of what they call "Norwich crape" or of "Bombazeen", which looks pretty, and is very durable wear. Sometimes may be seen a woman having an Indian silk shawl, and a Tuscan bonnet, which are thought superb. You may think their wardrobes are somewhat scanty, but we can assure you there is much pride amid all this, and young women then are thought very fine and richly dressed when in their best.

Let us next see how the people live, and what they eat and drink at this time. Their food is like their dress, what we should think the commonest fare. Very little white bread is seen in their houses, and it is not eaten much, except on Saturday, the baking day, and on Sunday. Flour is dear, and white bread scarce amongst the bulk of the people. The high price is caused by a heavy tax put upon all wheat coming from a foreign country. The English aristocracy, who are the large landowners, are the sole rulers, or makers of our laws, and they passed the Corn Laws for their own special benefit, to keep up their rents, though they must know by doing this they are pinching and starving millions of men, women, and children. Flesh meat is not much eaten by the masses of the working classes, they think themselves well off if they have plenty of pudding to dinner, very seldom is meat eaten before or after pudding, except on Sundays. Both flesh meat and many other things are looked upon by many as a luxury and fitter for the rich than for them. Some console themselves by saying that "bread and water are all that are promised, and the more people suffer in this world the more they will enjoy in the next." Oat-cake, brown bread, porridge pudding, skimmed milk, potatoes, and home-brewed beer, which they always call "drink", are the principal articles of food. Tea, coffee, and sugar are dear, butter is not much used, and treacle even is deemed a luxury! Most of the women and many girls can bake this oatcake, called "havver cake" or bread. It is baked on a "bakstone" (bakestone) built in bricks. Some have double bakstones on which two cakes can be baked at the same time. On these sometimes the neighbours bake in turns, taking their meal tubs and coal to heat the bakstone. In almost every house may be seen a *creel* consisting of cords attached to the joists over the hearth, on which the oatcake is hung to harden; also cakes made of wheaten flour, called "bread meal", are put on this creel for the same purpose, and they soon get so hard as to require good teeth, which happily the people as a rule possess. There is much art in baking this oatcake, some can always make it fine, thin, and crisp, while others make it thick and flinty. If a young woman can bake oatcake and brew well, it is thought she will make a good wife; but if she can do neither she is looked down upon as being very defective.

Brewing home-brewed beer, or "drink", is a great institution, and most women can do it, though they vary much in their efficiency and reputation. It requires an important plant, consisting of a variety of utensils, to brew. A vessel to boil the water in, a mash tub, brewing tub, hop tems and briggs, besides a funnel, barrels or "drink-pots", which cost too much for every poor family to have them all; hence few persons own a complete plant, so there is a deal of socialism or co-operation in connection with it in most neighbourhoods, some owning part, and others part, each having their brewing days to suit the convenience of the rest, and one can scarcely go into a neighbourhood without seeing these articles carried from one house to another. Malt and hops are sold at certain shops, where a small mill is kept, in which the buyer of malt grinds it. As we have hinted, women differ much in their ability to brew good drink. Some put the water too hot on the malt in mashing it, or they may "set it on"—that is, put the yeast into the liquor when too cold or too hot; they may "ding in"—that is, take from the top the first crop of yeast and stir it up again—at an improper time; or they may not "tun it", that is, put it into barrels or drink-pots when they ought. But a woman can always have a plausible excuse for blunders made in brewing, and seldom fails to make a good use of such if her drink is faulty. She puts the blame on either the malt, hop, yeast, or maybe on the barrel or drink-pot, which she had lent to Sally, or borrowed from her, and was assured was thoroughly clean and sweet and was not; it must be some fault of someone apart from her own mismanagement. Whatever may be the cause, one thing is certain—there is much difference in Betty's and Mally's drink even when the same malt, hops, and yeast are used by both, and the same quantity of drink made from them.

Some of the women are noted for always having nice yeast on their drink, all such have a ready demand for it, for there is no German yeast*. Then there is much lending and borrowing yeast to be paid back when the borrower brews, and the brewers in a neighbourhood make arrangements with each other to brew at stated times in turns, to accommodate each other with yeast, and brewing has often to be put off for want of yeast to "set on" with, and they borrow drink till they can brew. Persons some-

---

*When it was first introduced there was much prejudice against it.

times spend many hours in seeking yeast to brew or bake with. If they seek it in their own locality it is to borrow, if outside it is to buy. There is publichouse yeast, but most people prefer home-brewed yeast to it. Yes, the yeast question in these days is a most momentous one.

This drink is found less or more in every house, and one thing is certain—that it is free from the pernicious adulterations most of the ales and porters are subject to.

Many meals are made of this drink, with maybe a little oat-cake and meat dripping. Sometimes this cake, called "havver bread", is toasted and put into the drink. Of course, the latter varies much in strength, some making more gallons to the peck of malt than others; some make two kinds, small and strong; others use more hop, and like it bitter. The hospitality of Pudsey people is well known, and as regards this drink it is boundless. One can scarcely put his head into a house, or look in at a door or window, but he is asked to take a "sup of drink". The milk carrier and he who brings the "mule-load of coal" are asked to have a "sup of drink." On a winter's night, when neighbours meet to chat in all but total darkness, the host is certain to draw them "mugpots" of drink. If one is extra pleased or grieved he gets a "drop of drink". It is drunk by all, rich and poor, old and young, parson and cobbler, made extra strong for weddings, Christmas, and feasts, and sometimes warmed, sugared, and rum put in. People have no idea a person's health would be safe without it, and some Methodist class-leaders say they could not lead their classes without getting a "mugpot" of drink. It is taken for "forenoon drinkings", and as a substitute for tea at four in the afternoon; probably this is the reason why teas are called "drinkings" in Pudsey. One thing is certain, that this drink is supposed to contain more strength and nourishment than any other article, and fathers tell their children to "open their shoulders, and let it go down."

CHAPTER IV

Courtship and Love-Making

The villagers' knowledge of each other—Few means of meeting outsiders—Dangerous courting lasses in other villages—No love-letters, cheap trips, or galas—Leeds and Bradford fairs—Giving up courting in despair—Mock courtship for a purpose—Pudsey tide—A famine before and after—Abusing Pudsey people's hospitality—Shabby to leave home at Tide-time—How and where the Tide is held—The market for sweethearts—A "Tiding" a "God's-penny"—Lads and lasses at the alehouse—Village gossip—"Hearkening courters"—"Pitchering Brass"—Calling persons out of their names—Courting by proxy.

In those days, as we have said, nearly all the people of Pudsey know each other, unlike the inhabitants living in large towns and cities where the people are thrown together from different parts of the country, strangers to each other, many of them not knowing their next door neighbours. Nearly all the young lads and lasses of Pudsey know each other by sight if not by name, though mostly by the latter, more especially is it so in one's immediate neighbourhood, as an up-towner or down-towner; hence in choosing a wife there is no need to make much inquiry of any one respecting each other, as every character is very well known—though, of course, everyone has not the same good or bad opinion of everyone else, for they differ as to what constitutes a good character, just as they differ as to what is a beautiful face. Courtship, therefore, in this state of things, does not consist so much in making each other's acquaintance, as in keeping each other company as companions. This choosing of life partners is mostly confined to the same neighbourhood, as up-towners and down-towners. There is no such thing as writing love-letters! It is as well it is so: otherwise courting amongst the common or working people would be impossible, as a letter costs a half-day's wage; but there is no need of letter writing in making love, as the parties generally live near each other. There are no railways, and, of course, no cheap trips to places where the sexes may meet and form acquaintance with each other whose places of residence are far apart. No galas nor balls where the labouring classes meet and make new friends, joining in couples in polkas, quadrilles, or in waltzing, and which might result sometimes in unions for life. Nearly all journeys

are made on foot, and walking out is deemed a luxury. The people
are hedged round in their own and the few neighbouring villages,
where it is customary to visit the annual feasts, or maybe Leeds
or Bradford fairs, or to the last great show at Bradford, called
"Bishop Blaize", where many young couples went from the surrounding villages. But the people so seldom leave their homes,
or their own immediate localities, that narrow prejudices are
fostered, and if one man goes from one part of the village to
another to win a girl and make her his wife, he is looked upon
as an interloper by the young men there, and as a poacher on
their preserves, and is often badly treated. Many have to give
up in despair, after being covered with mud, and suffering much
bodily harm; while some persist, and brave all danger, and win
a wife; and in other cases it may be that though they have
failed in their suit, they have been the means of stimulating
some young man in the girl's locality, whose mind was previously undecided, to come forward and make the girl his wife,
having had his jealousy roused by the attention paid to her by
the outsider. We have heard of cases where a kind of understood
engagement had existed for years, but where the attachment of
the male lover was not ardent, where a man from the neighbouring locality, friendly to the girl, has attempted a mock
courtship and succeeded in warming the affections of the old
lover, which has speedily ended in a wedding. If a young man
ventures as far as Tong, or some other neighbouring village, in
search of a wife, as sometimes happens, those in his own village,
especially the women, are up in arms against such cosmo-
politanism; they tell him he might have got as good a girl, aye,
and a good deal better, at home. He is told that he is nearly
certain to "rue the day," and "make a bad bargain," while the
friends of the girl are saying the same about the Pudsey lad,
so these two are tormented both at home and abroad.

Pudsey feast is a great time for bringing people together,
especially courters, as well as for making love matches, and
deciding many who have not been able to decide during the year.
But feasts in those days were worth being called such. They were
real feasts. Let us picture to ourselves Pudsey feast nearly 60
years ago. There are few inhabitants 'tis true, but they do not
go to the seaside—they cannot get there; probably not one in a
hundred ever did, or ever will, see the ocean. Besides scarcely any
one could think of leaving the feast to go away. No, they all stay
at home. They have no objection to having a little off, but it must
not be at feast time, for, even if they asked no one, who knows
who might "pop in", as they call it, and how selfish it would
look, just as if they had gone off at "tide time" on purpose, lest

some relation or friend should drop in and have a "bit of beef." This would not be like Pudsey folks, hence most of them invite and expect visitors at feast time. Besides many of them actually owe some beef, for have they not been to several feasts even during this same year, and were well treated? And how shabby it would be to leave home and "lock up," as they say, when those whose houses they had visited would be coming expecting the same hospitality they had shown. Then this may be the only time during the year when many of them see each other, or at least when they can entertain them properly, for they are never so well prepared to offer them such lots of nice things as at feast time, because however scanty their fare may be at other times nearly everyone contrives by "hook or crook" to have a variety of good things for the feast. So what with the people staying at home, and so many outsiders coming into the village, there is a busy Pudsey "tide." We may add, while on this subject, that both visiting feasts and making preparations for them are carried to great excess. Many unreasonable and greedy persons, having but the slightest acquaintance with some Pudsey man or woman, come on the feast Sunday merely to *gormandise*, and maybe they bring others with them who are complete strangers to the host, and thus take undue advantage of the well-known hospitality of Pudsey folk. We have known cases where poor families have been literally eaten up on the Sunday by an influx of unexpected, and no doubt unwelcome, visitors, and had to fare badly themselves the remainder of the feast week. Many families are very foolish; they not only save up maybe for months for the feast, but get into debt as well for it, and some have bought more beef than they needed because it came easy, for their practice or custom is to get new and pay for old, always a year behindhand as regards payment. Of course the butcher secures them as customers for the year. There is much meaning in the saying that there is a "famine before and after a feast," for many suffer more or less throughout the year from a too lavish expenditure for the feast.

Our business, however, is to show the connection there is between a feast and love-making. Perhaps there is no great difference in feasts at one time and place and at another time and place. Not long before the time of which we speak, the feast was held on the moor or common, before that village playground was "taken in." Let us, however, go now to Chapeltown where the feast is held compact, and not divided in different parts of the village. It is Monday, and we see a variety of diversions and attractions, such as they are. Stalls, of course, with gingerbread and nuts (a feast would not be one without those two articles) and fruits in great variety; dolls, etc., for girls, and horses, drums, trumpets, whips, etc., for the boys. There are peep shows showing the Battle of Waterloo, etc., automatic figures going through theatrical performances, and the death of the Babes in the Wood, besides the everlasting Punch and Judy; and the swing boats, buckets, and whirligigs; also fat men, fat women, and fat pigs, and numerous gambling tables with dice and "Black cock or white," and there are the "knacks" for gambling, etc., as well as many rings of men formed tossing up coins, much money changing hands when they come down "heads or tails." At their homes up to 4 or 5 o'clock in the afternoon, friends are chatting with friends; most of the men are at the publichouse, playing skittles, brasses, or quoits; and eating and drinking is universal and almost perpetual. After tea, a large proportion of the people are seen wending their way to Chapeltown, parents to buy their children the long promised "tiding," and husbands to treat their wives. But this feast on Monday and Tuesday afternoons or evenings is the greatest time of the year for the young lads and lasses. The latter go dressed in their bit of best, and stand in massive groups in the feast, and it is said are anxiously waiting for sweethearts. This may be true, but if so it is nothing but right, legitimate, and fair—though some of them have an eye to someone they have a kind of sneaking, yet honourable, liking for, if the young man only knew it. Well, maybe he does, and reciprocates her attachment, but never has had the courage to make overtures. Others there are who agree to meet their lovers there, while the old courters meet and walk together to the feast. This is all right and decent, and as it should be. The lads get among the lasses, passing familiar jokes; some of them behave rather rudely, such may have been at the alehouse drinking during the day. If a young man prevails upon a young woman to accept of a "tiding," which means accepting brandy-snap and nuts, the ice is broken, and it is mostly looked upon by old and young as a kind of "God's penny," for the girl feels laid under some obligation to him; it is a proof that they are making love to each other if not actually engaged. But if she consents to go with him to the publichouse, where there are a variety of attractions, mingled, we are sorry to say, with much drunkenness, it is considered a double proof that they are both in earnest and mean business.

The public houses at feast times are places of great resort for the people, and during the Monday and Tuesday, and even on Sunday evening, almost every one is crowded with young couples, and so far as the young men are concerned, seldom do we hear any complaint made about them getting drunk at feast time.

Many married couples are seen there also, who seldom go at any other time. Sometimes the country dance is indulged in, though performed rather clumsily; single step is most common, or what is called a reel, danced by threes. Late in the evening they leave for home, walking together in couples. Those who are together for the first time are very shy of the public gaze, and as everyone knows everybody else, there are lots of people, both old and young, watching to see new pairs for the morrow's news and gossip. But one thing is in the lads' and lasses' favour; as before stated, there is no gas, no street lamps, and very little light shown from the dwellings, so unless it is a clear moonlight night, they are somewhat protected, and avoid much of the vulgar intrusion of these busybodies. There is one great drawback however; rude and insolent boys, and others too old to be called such, hide in secret places, and listen to what the young couples may say, and then noise it abroad the next day throughout the neighbourhood. This practice is a kind of profession with some, and is called "harkening courters," and frequently these people are not content with telling what they heard, but make many cruel additions, so that what is said in secret, and maybe in a whisper, is proclaimed as from the house top. A Pudsey tide, or feast, in these days is an important occasion, and looked forward to by scores of young men and young women as one which will probably decide their fortunes for life. It is a kind of love market, where if there is a brisk demand for the lasses, the lads from fear of losing their chances sometimes seize their prizes. While on the other hand, should the market be rather slack for them, some girls consent to go with a young man who for some time had been pressing his attentions but had never been able to succeed. Most of the courting is done out of doors, and standing outside on cold winter nights has caused many to suffer in their health, and in some cases death has resulted. It is a foolish custom, and ought to be avoided.

A custom very prevalent is for parties to "pitcher" courters. They go to them when standing together, and tell them that they want the "pitchering brass," holding a pitcher or jug, and if not paid they have no rest, but are constantly annoyed, and maybe sodded in the dark, or water thrown onto them, and perhaps cruelly beaten, etc. But if they pay their "pitchering" they are protected ever after. Should they pay it, the money is spent in drinks of some kind.

Then what gossip there is, especially among the women folks, when weddings are to come off! Some say they don't know what Sally can see in Jack, or Nanny in Ben, or Bet in Bob. There's mostly two sides, and sometimes more; for others, friendly to

the lads, think both Jack, Ben, and Bob, are as good as Sally,
Nanny, and Bet; others think they are better; while others think
they are very well matched. You may think it strange that nearly
all in the village have a name very different to the one given
them by their godfathers and godmothers when christened.
Speaking of the male sex,

> It's Bill, and Jack, and Ned,
> And Doss, and Doze, and Fred,
> And Dawd, and Dont, and Ike,
> With Ben, and Tom, and Mike.
> Sometimes the last is Mick,
> And then there's Dan and Dick,
> With Bob, Math, Abe, and Jim,
> And Kit, Jer, Sam, and Tim.

While with the women folks,

> It's Susy, Ailsy, and Tet,
> Or Peggy, and Matty, and Bet,
> There's Milly, and Becca, and Dolly,
> And Meacy, as well as Polly.
> There's Pally, or some say Mally,
> And Hetta, Jenny, and Sally,
> There's Bessy or Bess, Sue, and Fan,
> With Liddy, Nanny or Nan.

It may seem strange that parents after being at so much
trouble, as some of them are at times, to find names for their
children before christening them, should start directly they
leave the church to call them something else, for, as a rule, children are called by others what they are called at home.

Married women with all their little gossip are very useful in
getting the lads and lasses together. They plead their cause
and help them to overcome many difficulties. They have a larger
experience than the young folks, and perform both for them and
society at large very important and beneficial service. They invite the opposite sexes to tea sometimes and speak a good word
for their favourites. In fact, it may be said, and said truly, that
a very large share of the courting is done by the married women,
and even the old women do a large amount of work of this sort
sometimes, for we know cases where matters of courtship have
been made smooth and agreeable by the wise and shrewd diplo-
macy of some old woman.

CHAPTER V

Old Time Weddings

Love-making not confined to the feast-time—Old time lanes
and fields—Going to Tong Church and Fulneck Chapel under
false pretences—Pudsey on a certain day—All astir—Two weddings—Walking to Calverley Church—Gossip and Bridescake—
Following the Weddings—"Chalking up a Shot"—Throwing away
money for luck—"Sodding the Weddingers"—The "Enbrass"—
A Riding Wedding—The dowry, and wedding presents.

Before making a few remarks on old time weddings at Pudsey,
we wish it to be understood that what has been said on courtship and love-making at feast time, was not intended to produce
the impression that they were confined to this great annual holiday, but that it was one of the most important occasions for that
kind of business; though the interchange of soft words, tender
endearments, and caresses between the lads and lasses of Pudsey
(more or less) took place all the year round. At the time of which
we are speaking, nearly sixty years ago, the village and its neighbourhood was more favourable for love-making than it is today,
for there were no cheap day trips by railway to the seaside, and
other places, or galas for dancing and promenading, short Satur-
days or Bank-holidays, the village streets or lanes were more
secluded, and larks could be seen soaring o'er one's head, trilling
their joyous songs in any part of the village over fields close by.
The fields with their footpaths then were worth calling fields,
more hedgerows and fewer stone fences, and the woods adjoining
were real ones, and not poor imitations as now, and even in
the centre of the village was a nice little sylvan shade called
Crawshaw Wood. There were pleasant secluded walks in every
part, through fields and woods, or beside the running brooks and
murmuring becks, where young women might be seen in groups,
and a cluster of as many young men might be seen following in
their track, flinging their harmless jokes at each other, and often
whispering words of entreatment and admiration. All this might
be seen on a Sunday morning, but more so on a Sunday evening,
in spring time, when the leaves and buds were bursting fresh and
green, and the primrose showed its cheerful countenance, as well
also in summer and autumn, through fields of new-mown hay

and waving golden corn, or beside or through woods where the
songs of the linnet, blackbird and thrush, were sung out in rich
and mellow notes, or along green lanes, where they gathered
hawthorn blossom, the wild rose, or sweet honeysuckle. We have
known many cases of young women who would get leave from
their parents to go to Tong Church or Fulneck Chapel, which
were only plausible excuses for meeting some young man there
for whom they had a harmless fondness, and we have sympa-
thised with their object considerably. In addition to these young
men and women, might be seen older courters walking in
couples—on the point of wedding—their courting nearly done.
These walked at a more loitering pace, theirs being a more
steady, settled and well-understood business, and a stranger
would not be able to tell from their demeanour, whether they
were courters, or man and wife. In fact such were wed, except
the outward ceremony at church to tell the outside world.

With the above concluding remarks on Courtship and Love-
making, let us look at Pudsey as it appeared on a certain day
nearly sixty years ago. The village is all astir, and there seems to
be joy in the very air. What is there up? And what are so many
villagers standing at their doors, or in groups and clusters, talking
about, and looking out for with such expectation? All seem on
"tip toe," stretching their necks, looking in one direction, as if
to catch the sight of something unusual. It cannot be to see the
expected funeral of some well-known villager, who is to be carried
to his, or her, final resting place—they are too jovial and gay for
that. Let us mingle with the people and inquire, and what do we
learn? Why, that there are two weddings today, both in that
neighbourhood, and they are waiting to see them pass! The spectators know that the weddings come off today, for they have been
"spurred three times," which means the banns have been published; they also know the rings have been bought, and the
bridecakes made. Some know all the wedding guests, and how,
or in what way, many of the young lasses are to be dressed,
having seen the material at the dressmakers; another knows
who made the bride's cake, and has actually tasted it. One in the
group, an apparently shrewd woman, has doubts as to whether
Bob, the name of one to be married, will make his appearance,
for he and Nanny have been spurred before, and Bob failed to
come forward, and she says that he is "bad to catch." Both the
weddings have to pass this way, so let us walk nearer the first
wedding house. Now we see a crowd of men, women, boys and
girls, and learn that all the men have had their breakfasts at the
bridegroom's father's house, rum possit, etc., which is customary,
and have each fetched their lover or partner from her father's

house. The crowd gets impatient, for it is late in the forenoon,
and they have to walk to Calverley Church and cannot be married
after twelve o'clock at noon. There is a move—they leave the
house at last, and form in couples, each lad with a lass holding
by his arm; the second wedding is in view, all is excitement; the
crowds gather round for bridecake, which is handed to friends or
scattered amongst the crowd; some of the bystanders make remarks to the weddingers, and get replies; the brides are told to
hold up their "heads" and keep their spirits up, and the bride-
grooms are told by the married they are going to the land of
"Uz," meaning the married land or state.

Now this is a "walking wedding," as it is called, and means
simply what they call it; they walk, as nearly all do at this time,
in couples to Calverley and back. But why to Calverley? Because
the Vicar has the monopoly of all the weddings in the parish.
Dissenting ministers in the eye of the law and the State Church
are quacks, and persons would be living in a state of adultery
or fornication if the wedding ceremony was performed by them.
But see what a large number of men in blue smocks are following
the two weddings! It is customary for lots to walk after weddings
to the public house near Calverley Church, for there's mostly a
chance of getting ale, etc., to be paid for by the wedding parties,
and being *two* weddings today there will be a chance of getting
more; these kind of "camp followers" often manage to chalk up
a good *shot* or *score*, before the marriage ceremony is over. After
the weddingers emerge from the Church, they throw a sum of
money over their heads amongst a crowd of men, women and
boys, not to do which would be unlucky. They are not supposed
to know the exact sum, and the people rush to get a good share of
the scramble. The drunkenness at these weddings is very bad
sometimes. And few even of the most pious men are heard to
make complaints. After being at the alehouse near the Church
and frequently urged by the young women to leave for home,
they form in couples, and the custom is to throw sods at them.
Some in the village (Pudsey) may be seen with piles of sods
waiting for the return of the weddingers. Sods at that time could
be got in almost any of the streets, and if not there was always
a field not far off; and we have often seen much damage done to
lasses' dresses and men covered with mud in wet weather, and
worse still, serious injuries sustained by some in the eyes and
face. The wedding parties, ten couples in all, go to the wedding
houses to dine, where such as are tolerably sober have a chance
of dining well, though it too frequently happens that many of
the male sex are anything but that, and have to be held up by
their partners all the way from Calverley; while many decent

people, in every other respect, may be heard saying "It is a poor heart that never rejoices," though what joy there can be in a person drinking ale or spirits till he is sick and unable to stand upright or steady and has to be borne up by a young woman, we cannot understand.

The following morning a reliable friend waits upon the newly-married parties to receive the "enbrass," or as Chaucer gives it, "enbrase," meaning embrace, which is a sum of money according to the man's ability or disposition, and all the wedding parties go about the village inviting women to tea, and male friends to the "enbrass" at some public house. Those invited pay perhaps a shilling each, with which the, say, sovereign received, is spent in drinks. All the parties go in couples there during the evening, and dancing and singing is engaged in, and lots of fun and frolic; many songs are sung which we should think indecent, but not thought so then. Here again there is mostly much drunkenness. The honeymoon is spent at home, in both bride and bridegroom working to buy a little furniture for housekeeping, very few people being able to furnish when they wed, but mostly live for some time with the girl's father. We speak, of course, now of the bulk of the working people in Pudsey at that time.

We will add a few words respecting another kind of wedding, amongst a rather richer sort of folks, who have a "riding wedding," but none of your railways, 'buses, cabs, carriages or shandredans; the riders are all on horseback, single horse and double, one on some, and two on others, a lass behind her lover. Such weddings as these mostly consist of persons who keep a horse in their business, or at least can ride a horse. Our remarks already made apply in nearly all respects to this sort of wedding, also, except that from drunkenness and furious galloping more accidents occur. It is deemed a great honour for a rider to out-race the rest, and fetch the silver (oftener pewter) tankard containing ale and rum, or pure spirits, with a ribbon tied to the handle, and to go back to meet the rest to let them drink. There is great racing on the road, and they may be seen coming home from Calverley through the village at great speed, the horses whipped and spurred, sweating and foaming; many tumble off, and there is great risk in turning an abrupt corner at full speed, and especially if, as often is the case, the rider is drunk. Sometimes a young woman may be seen riding alone, for there are a few who can ride a horse well at this time. We ought to have said that all the young men at the walking weddings tie round their hats various coloured ribbons, and very little is thought of a wedding if there is a poor show of ribbons on the hats; such are called shabby.

What a difference there is with regard to a working man's wedding in Pudsey, at the time referred to, and one in a large town! No-one notices the latter, because so common, and besides the people are not known as in a small village where all know each other. Pudsey, as it increases in population, will make it impossible for its inhabitants to know each other, and their private circumstances as well as when the people were few. There is one important matter we had forgot, viz., the "dowry" which it is common for a working man to get with his wife, and which is mostly a rolling-pin, baking-spittle, pincushion, and sometimes a family Bible, rather expensive in those days; or it might be a few pots, bowls, or stool chair, corner cupboard, or some other useful article, and it is considered a famous affair if her "dowry" should be a "kist" or bedstead. Wedding presents (if any) consist of small, but useful, articles, and what more can be expected from a people possessing such scanty means as the bulk of them did sixty years ago?

CHAPTER VI

What is the Chief Employment?

Weaving cotton on hand-looms—Power-looms supersede them—
Making of woollen cloths—Hand-looms—Jennies, etc.—"Lead-
houses" and wool dyeing—Drying wool and tentering pieces out
of doors—"Moiting" wool by hand—"Lecking pieces"—Clothmakers going to Leeds market—Their talk at the Inns on the
road—"Wetting Bobbins" with a "sahker"—Revolution caused by
the "Bobbin sinker"—Hand-loom weaving has its drawbacks.

Our purpose is not to give a particular and minute account of
the chief employment of the people of Pudsey, which is well-
known to have been the making of woollen cloths. We have no
intention of noticing step by step the various changes and improvements in that branch, with a particular description of the
various machines, their inventors, and the persons' names who
first adopted them, etc. Our object is to give a general sketch,
consisting for the most part of what we ourselves have witnessed,
what we have seen and heard; so that all who choose to read
what we may pen may be able to compare Pudsey half a century,
or more ago, with today, and see the changes which have taken
place. Those who wish to see a more detailed and laboured account
of many things we may deal with, should not fail to see a work
to be issued shortly by Mr. Smith, of Morley, on "Morley Ancient
and Modern." We have just read that gentleman's prospectus, and
from the synopsis of its contents, we think it will be a most
interesting work, and in many respects in the woollen branch will
be applicable to Pudsey; while Mr. S. Rayner has contributed at
various times much valuable information on the ancient history
of Pudsey. To deal with the general features of Pudsey and its
people during the last sixty years, to describe them as they
appeared to us, to see the people in their homes, what they have
been doing and thinking, is our intention, and by doing this
young people can hardly help seeing that great changes have
taken place, and not mere change, but improvement as well.

Sixty years ago, in passing through the village of Pudsey,
especially the upper parts of it, we hear slight but rapid tappings
or rappings in the houses, made by the flying shuttles of the
hand-loom weavers of cotton. There are also some weaving
worsteds, though we are not aware that any of the cotton manufacturers reside in the village, the warps are put out by agents,

and the pieces are taken in and paid for by them. The weavers
in some cases are men, but mostly women, girls and boys, and the
looms may be seen in the houses where they live as we pass along.
But we soon see these cotton looms taken down, and in most
cases hand looms for weaving woollen cloth put in their places.
The making of woollen cloth has long been the chief employment
of the villagers, though of a crude sort of cloth. In the cotton
branch power-looms are superseding the hand-looms, in spite of
the determined opposition of the hand-loom weavers, who at
Blackburn destroyed more than a thousand in one week, and at
Shipley a power-loom for weaving worsted is dragged through
the street and destroyed. The cloth made at this time in Pudsey
is mostly made of coarse wool, thick spun and woven in an open
"set," or gears and slays. In Leeds a finer wool is made up into
better cloths, though Leeds is noted for its stuff manufactures,
whose merchants attend the Bradford and Halifax markets to
sell their goods. It is not long since the picking stick and flying
shuttle were introduced. Our fathers tell us of seeing persons
throw the shuttle with their hand through the shed or sheard,
or of two persons when the cloth was broader weaving on one
loom. They also tell us of seeing carding done by hand, and the
yarn being spun a single thread at a time on a spinning wheel.
There are spinning jennies now, one with 50 spindles is considered
a great affair; there are many 38 spindles, and we have spun on
one of that count for days together nearly twenty years after
the time we are speaking of. Nearly sixty years ago, some of the
people walked to Bramley, Armley, Farnley and Wortley, backwards and forwards, every day, to weave or spin; others work at
manufacturers' houses in the village; while others have looms in
the chambers over where they live, and get work from makers in
slubbing coppings from the slubbers at the mills, which they draw
out on the jennies into warp and weft, and weave into cloth on
their hand-looms.

The clothmakers are a hardworking resolute sort of folks, and
we have heard one tell how he had fetched a pack of wool on
his back from Halifax, and "litted," that is, dyed, it the same day,
and that it was not uncommon for persons to do it. Places for
dyeing, called lea'dhouses, are to be seen throughout the village,
and many woollen manufacturers have one on their own
premises. The wool is mostly dried out of doors, as are cloths,
on tenters. When the spinning jennies were first introduced you
should have been there and seen and heard the people, or some
of them—the more conservative sort of folks who always dread
a change. They are lamenting and downcast; "England is ruined,
one man will do the work of ten, and get very little more for it,"

they say, and that there will not be half work for the people in the future. At first all yarns were spun into coppings, the weft about half the twist of the warp, and the former is still wound on to bobbins on the one spindled wheel ready for the weaver's shuttle, and we have seen the winders, who are mostly women, girls, and boys, with the blood dropping off their fingers, caused by the friction of the yarn in winding these bobbins. In a while, we see a great change. Wires are put round the jenny spindles to hold the bobbins by the staples, and prevent them being loose, and to make them go round with the spindle, and thus supersede the winding on the bobbin wheel. Then we hear another general outcry made—that what with one thing and another, there is going to be nothing to do for people soon but to "pine" (starve) to death. There are some who after all stick to the winding on the wheel, their fathers and mothers had done so, and it must be best. A time comes, however, when they give way, and acknowledge the jenny an institution which is quite constitutional.

Some of the wool used has many burrs and "moits" (as motes are called) in it, and a large number of women and children fetch it, a stone at a time, to moit, for there are no burring or moiting machines to take them out. Weavers have to wet or "leck" the pieces when woven by putting on a liquid to scour or wash out the grease, etc., at the mill, and it is quite common to see weavers carry these pieces full of not a very sweet liquid on their backs, or in a wheelbarrow. It requires a rather expensive plant for a poor weaver to prepare the liquid required, but they lend and borrow amongst each other.

You would be amused to hear many of the tales, anecdotes, and conversations of these old-time clothmakers, not only as told and heard at the publichouses in the village, but as they go to and fro to the market in the Cloth Hall, Leeds, in groups, especially when walking home at nights, calling at well-known alehouses on the road to have a "sup of something to drink." We could mention names if necessary to do so, but some of them are not sufficiently ancient for that. Anyone, however, who is wishful to know them may easily do so by looking into Baines' Directory, published in 1822, where the name of each clothmaker appears with the inn he stopped at in Leeds. They "spin their yarns"—telling what they have sold and what they have to sell, what price they have got that day, what the merchant who bought the cloth said, and what he, the maker, said to him. They have no secret in the manufacturing, are not afraid of others getting their styles and patterns, all is fair and above board, as they are nearly all making similar goods. If they have sold off all their goods, and realised a good profit, they get an

extra glass, and probably treat the company, and in the exuber-
ance of intoxicated joy they think themselves richer than they
really are, and boast openly of being richer and having more
"brass" than all the lot of them, and could buy them all up, etc.,
when probably if living today no one would consider them rich
at all, though, relatively speaking, they might be at the time
referred to. The poor were poorer than now, so that a man who
could make as much cloth as employed his own family only,
would be considered rich. There is a deep meaning in this idea,
and much truth, for what independence a man feels who can
employ himself, and not be compelled to ask another for work
to enable him to live! Seeking and asking, and almost begging
and praying, for work to save one from starvation, is one of the
most humiliating sights one can imagine, and we have known
persons whose greatest ambition was to be a woollen manufacturer in order to be able to employ himself and his family, so
as to be saved from the degradation of asking others not only his
equals, but in many cases far below him in everything that constitutes good character, to allow him to live. Many of these old-
time clothiers are men of this sort, and only make sufficient to
employ themselves and families. Some have a few outside looms,
but there are few large manufacturers; and many now with the
great productive powers they possess—the result of the many
improvements in machinery during even the last thirty years—
are able to make as much profit from their large production or
turnover in almost any year as our old manufacturers would
have made *if the cost of all they manufactured had been profit!*

Before concluding this letter we will refer to a matter which
some may think of small importance, but it is in reality a most
momentous one, trivial as some may think it, involving on a small
scale quite a revolution in connection with the business of a
hand-loom weaver, *viz.*, that of

"WETTING BOBBINS"

The loose fibres of the weft prevented it coming off the bobbin
in going across the warp, except it was wet with water, which
was also necessary to enable the weaver to "get his weft in," by
making the shots, called "shoits," lay close to each other to make
a firm cloth. Each bobbin of weft had to be thoroughly soaked
in water; after which a number of them were piled on each other
in what was called a "siper," to drain the bulk of the water out.
This siper was made in the form of a V. The old mode of wetting
bobbins was as follows: The weaver had a bowl or some other
vessel of water under the siper, into which he put his bobbins,
and taking one at a time he held it under the water with his
left hand, having in his right hand a wooden tube called a

"bobbin sahker," meaning sucker, to which he applied his mouth, placing the lower end of the tube close against the weft on the bobbin under water, and then sucked or withdrew the air, so as to cause the water to thoroughly soak the weft; but if from any mismanagement the tube was not placed properly on the bobbin, the dirty water would rush into the weaver's mouth, which was a common occurrence, and what made this an aggravated calamity was that sometimes very disagreeable ingredients were in this bobbin water, from which arose an offensive odour. Then in winter time the water was frequently either frozen or within a few degrees of frost, when this process with one hand in the water was performed, which made it a cold job.

Well, there came a time which produced quite a revolution in the mode of wetting bobbins. Someone invented an instrument to supersede the bobbin "sahker," for from time immemorial there have been men who were not satisfied with things as they were, especially if they got it into their heads that things as they were could be improved. This has always been the case, and probably always will be to the end of time. This new invention was not called a "bobbin sahker," because it was not one, but a "bobbin sinker," which it was. It was founded on the principle of a pump, or a boy's squirt, made of tin, and so shaped at the bottom end as to cover the bobbin of weft, which was held under water, and the air was displaced by pulling up a wooden stopper wrapped with weft to fill the tin tube, by which simple process the bobbin of weft was saturated with water. There was great rejoicing by men of progress when they first saw this bobbin sinker, for in it they saw a great deliverance from considerable difficulty and annoyance caused by the old bobbin "sahker." But here again was manifested the old conservative element, persons opposed to all change, except the raising of weaving a penny or twopence per string. They protested against the new-fangled notion of a bobbin sinker, and stuck to the old "sahker," as they probably would to their mothers' breasts had they been allowed to do so. These went on in the old way till they either died off or sulkily took to the new improvements for wetting bobbins.

Hand-loom weaving, with a good warp and good weft, and not too much of the latter to put in, with constant work and double the price they got for weaving, would not be an objectionable business. The weaver was under shelter, and not exposed as some outdoor labourers were. Weavers had much freedom, could work short hours and make it up when convenient, not being "called to labour by a bell." But the hand-loom weaver had many drawbacks—many difficulties, trials, and much tribulation, as we shall try to show in our next article.

CHAPTER VII

The Trials and Difficulties of Hand-Loom Weavers

Cloth-makers become numerous—Panics and bad-times—Small manufacturers—Few weavers and spinners have constant work—Seeking work—Bad customs "Odd jobbing" or working for nothing—Waiting for slubbing—Sizing, and "Laking for druft"—Putting webs out to dry—Seeking gears—Power-looms dreaded—Effects of machinery—"Open-band and cross-band"—Difficulty in making cloths alike.

From the time of which we have been speaking, the population of Pudsey continued to increase, and small woollen manufacturers became more numerous, when a different class of goods began to be made in a greater variety, but much less durable in wearing, finer spun, and woven in finer gears and slays. Amongst all the changes, or mixed up with them, both in the old and new state of things, there were bad times, when the working classes were sorely tried and at their "wits' end" to get sufficient porridge and bread. With all our present "depressed trade" we know comparatively nothing of what the people experienced in what some foolishly call the "good old times." Were it within our present province, it would be easy to write a good-sized volume on the constantly recurring panics and bad times, such as when the manufacturers of Huddersfield told Parliament that thirteen thousand people in the fancy trade were working for twopence-halfpenny per day, and paying for the wear and tear of their looms out of it! The suffering of the people, not only in Pudsey, but in almost every part of the country, both in the various manufacturing and the agricultural districts, was beyond all adequate description during the first half of the present century.

But apart from these frequent times of acute suffering, this change in the class of woollen goods made at Pudsey did not in the best of times make it an easy matter for the hand-loom weavers to get along; they had many trials and difficulties to contend with. There were very few who could depend on constant work (even when trade was not bad) from any of the manufacturers. Of course there were a few of the largest makers who were able to supply something like regular work, but such cases were rare. Few weavers knew when they got a piece to make for whom they would be spinning and weaving the next.

The bad customs we may enumerate in connection with cloth-making were more common, we believe, in the upper part of the village than the lower, *though far too prevalent in all parts*. The manufacturers, being mostly small capitalists, had often to sell one lot before they could make another, being, as it was said, "from hand to mouth." Some of them would frankly tell their men this, and urge them on, so that they might be able to buy more wool and the men have more work. It was quite common when trade was not bad to see weavers and spinners going from place to place seeking work, or to get a piece of cloth to make. If they succeeded it was mostly on the condition that they helped to break the wool for it; that is, opened the bales, then the fleeces, taking off the coarse parts called the *britch*, put it in sheets, then go to the mill and help to scour it, then "lit," or dye it, and the morning after take it out of the dye-pans into sheets ready for the dryhouse. If to dye black, then the wool had to be *soured*, that is, a foundation for the colour given it ready for dyeing the day following. All this was for *nothing*, except in some cases a small allowance for a little ale or cheese and bread. If the wool was taken to Leeds to dye indigo-blue, then it was only to open and britch, and to be looked over, that is, all the white bits taken out or lumps of tar cut off locks when it came from the dyehouse. However, after doing all this work, the weaver did feel somewhat relieved, knowing he had a claim now to a share in working it up when he could get a set of slubs to be spinning a web on the jenny. The small manufacturers sometimes put all the blend out in single pieces, that is, single webs (but mostly in *cloaths*, two web lots) as he wanted to have the cloth as soon as possible to market. When the slubber had doffed the first set of slubbing, it often became a serious question as to whose turn it was to have it, and casting lots would frequently be the mode of deciding it, for it was common for several weavers or spinners to be there waiting for it, and sometimes all the slubbing for the warps would be fetched from the mill in odd sets as doffed. Probably the weaver would be waiting of the warp being spun for his web, or the warper for the warp to warp. All this working for nothing and waiting took up time, while rents, rates, coal, and grocery bills were being run up. Then lists for the cloth's selvidge had to be laid up at the master's house, and sometimes there was waiting there either for the listing or their turn on the bartrees. When the web was warped there was the sizing process to go through, and the weavers, as a rule, had to buy their own size, though customs varied very much with different manufacturers in the village—there was nothing like uniformity in either wages or customs, which was a great drawback to both weavers and spinners. Well, the weaver might have to wait for his size at the sizing boilers, and the size varied in strength, or if not, the webs varied in their taking or absorbing it, and it was common for weavers to ask advice from their neighbours, and sometimes a little Size Conference might be seen deliberating as to which size-pot would be safest to pull the web through; while at other times if there was no suitable pot, or the web was very tender, the weaver would wring the size out of the web (after possing it) with his hands—rather tedious work, and requiring good judgment to do it all alike. This sizing business was an important affair, for on its being done properly or otherwise most serious results depended. If a web got a soft size, that is too little in it, the warp would chafe in the gears and slays, and flour was sometimes put on to make it work; while if too hard-sized, water had to be spurted on to it behind the gears.

After sizing the web, one of the most critical of all the processes is to put it out of doors to dry, for in a climate like ours the weather, especially at some seasons, is very fickle. A place is chosen, the web-sticks or stretchers are put out, and if frosty, a pick-axe is used to make holes in the ground for posts to hold the ends of the web, and a maul to drive them down. Sometimes might be seen a man and his wife up to their knees in snow going out with a web to dry, she carrying the web-sticks and her husband the wet web. This reminds me of a lecturer coming up, we think it was, Swinnow; a woman was carrying web-sticks, etc., which are not very easy for a woman to carry, and someone shouted out to him, "Hug 'er 'em, wi' tah." The stranger, a highly-educated man, wished to know the meaning of that expression, and was much amused when told it meant "carry them for her, wilt thou!"

Well, in winter time and when fine weather is scarce, webs get only partly dried, and have to be hung before the house or stove fire to finish; but it is quite a common thing to see a number of weavers who say they are "laking for druft," that is, waiting for fine weather to dry their webs. Yes, "druft," as it was called, was a most momentous matter with the hand-loom weavers. The next thing was the sort of gear and slay he must have, and owing to the sets having begun to vary so much, it was seldom that the same set could be used many times in succession. Gears and slays were rather expensive for a weaver, and they had mostly to find their own; therefore there was much lending and borrowing of gears. It was a common thing to see weavers who had been for hours, and in some cases a day or two, trying to borrow gears, five, six, and, some odd times, it might be a seven, portif quarter gear, nine to ten or eleven quarters wide, etc., as the case happened to be. Part Spanish wool was used, which had many burrs in it, and a deal of what was called "moity wark" was the result. Australian wool had not come fairly into use for woollens then, and these burrs, etc., gave the weavers much trouble, and having but a very bad light, there being no gas still, candles and oil lamps were used, some preferring the one, and some the other. Often might be seen a boy or girl, or perhaps a weaver's wife, standing on one side of the loom watching to see when a thread broke down, whilst the weaver watched the other side, because if a thread broke, and another "shoit" was picked, a dozen more might be broken. Then there was much poor work caused by uneven slubbing, which made a bad thread; by "twitty" warp, that is the thread having very small places in it, which soon broke; caused also sometimes by spinning smaller or finer than the quality of the wool warranted; besides burry wool would prevent the weft from coming off the bobbin, and gave the weaver trouble. The overlookers who scribbled and carded the wool, often spoiled it, and many weavers, as well as masters, had to suffer from that. Let us now suppose the weaver has "felled," that is finished, weaving his web. The next thing to be done was to "leck" or wet it, as before explained, ready for the carrier to take it to the mill to be scoured. When fulled or milled, as they called it, there was tentering. Probably now it would be done in the tenter-house, which was made almost as hot as an oven, if on the day before Leeds market, and when dried the cloth had to be "teemed," which means being taken off and laid on the grass to get the dew, and pulled along to clean it, to give a proper *handle* or *touch* to the merchant. The night might be in winter, cold and chilly, especially to persons who had come out of the hot tenter-house. After standing out with the cloth a proper time to catch sufficient dew, it had to be listed and cuttled, and put under a weight ready for the carrier taking it to Leeds market the following day. Many cases of sickness occurred amongst the weavers, and some deaths, caused by this exposure in dewing cloth. All this odd jobbing, we say, was done for nothing, and the wages paid for weaving and spinning alone, without doing all this in at the bargain, were very poor indeed. Some said that if these bad customs went on at the rate they had done, getting worse and worse every year, in the end weavers would have to find the manufacturers headings, lists, and gigbits before they could get a piece to make, and if some in our day think that hand-loom weavers had not sufficient tribulation in those days, we have only to say to such that had they been compelled to do what those weavers did their opinions would have been considerably modified. In addition to all this, what were called "outside makers" had considerable expense in the first outlay for looms, jennies, and bartrees, etc., such as shuttles, pickers, and all wear and tear, as well as rent for the loom, light and fuel in winter. Some of those outside makers, that is persons who had looms at home, and got slubbing to make up from the masters, had four looms, and it took the principal nearly all his time to do the "odd jobbing" for them, and we cannot wonder that a hand-loom weaver came to be called a "poverty knocker." It was no uncommon thing, too, when the work was done for the weavers to be unable to get paid for some time after, which often caused much disappointment, inconvenience, and suffering. As to the prices paid for weaving and spinning, some idea may be got from the fact that a certain class of goods was made called *petershams,* for which only twenty-one shillings—and in some cases only a pound—was paid, for fetching the slubbing from the mill, spinning it into warp and weft, warping the web, sizing, looming and weaving it into cloth—which, in many cases, took a man a fortnight to accomplish. Such was the condition of things when power-looms first began to be introduced, and while many were lamenting and complaining, we always said that things could not well be worse, and that there was one consolation—power-looms could not break the wool, nor seek work, nor scour, dye, fetch slubbing, warp lists, size and dry webs, seek gears or pay for them, "leck" pieces, and carry them to the mill, tenter, "teem," or dew and cuttle them. We said we wished everything was done by power, or machinery, from buying, selling, and designing, to book-keeping, so that the people had nothing to do but read, think, write, study nature, sketch or draw, travel, and recreate themselves by some rational and innocent amusement, for that even then the masses of the people at that time could hardly help getting a better share in the distribution of wealth, as machinery could not eat and drink all it produced, nor could a few capitalists. We still believe there is some truth in this, if not strictly so, and that just in proportion as machinery is adopted, though during the transition people whose labour is superseded will suffer more or less, ultimately will society be benefited, and get a larger share of needful things, though it may not be a proportionate share with the large capitalists who may be able rapidly to heap up large fortunes. It may easily be seen that the above rude, unjust, and oppressive customs were "penny wise and pound foolish," for the work done for nothing could not be possibly done, particularly some of it, as well as if done by men specially devoting all their time to such, as came to be the case ultimately.

In concluding this letter, it may not be amiss to mention a few difficulties and inconveniences to which both masters, spinners, and weavers were subject. All work was put out to make in a certain number of warterns of slubbing for each two or four ends of cloth. A wartern meant six pounds, and if a blend of wool yielded less weight of slubbing than was expected it was a serious matter for a small manufacturer, making sometimes all the difference of a profit or loss. Hence such were very anxious about the yield of slubbing, and an old friend of mine tells a story in his own experience as to what happened when he first began to make cloth for himself. He was much disappointed in the weight of slubbing he got, it being much less than he expected, and on the Sunday, though a very devout Methodist at the time, in spite of all he could do during singing, praying, and the sermon, this short weight constantly forced itself on his mind. During all that Sunday, whatever he might be doing and wherever he might be there rung in his ears his short weight, which, if we remember rightly, was "twenty-six warterns and two pund." Yes, the weight of slubbing was a most important consideration, and liable to upset all previous calculations, for short weight meant fewer strings and fewer yards of cloth to sell. Spinners had often to stop spinning warps till the weight of slubbing could be ascertained, or "bribes" had to be made, which was quite common. This means that a different kind of weft had to be used to "fell" or finish the web. These bribes were quite common; and many persons, mostly manufacturers, might be seen with one thrown over their shoulders as substitutes for overcoats, even in going to Leeds market.

Again, under the old system of jennies and hand-looms cloth could not be made as uniform. If the work was not so good the spinner would perhaps spin the warp thicker to make a stronger thread, and would have less weft, which he might spin a little smaller or finer. Sometimes the web was warped a portiff or two narrower to make up for the thick spinning, and if one weaver acted according to orders and another took liberties, the ends would not mill together in the stock; one proving broader or shorter than the other. Then some spinner would give his warp more twist than another, and same by the weft, and this would affect the milling or fulling in the stocks.

After a while manufacturers had the slubbing for warp twisted one way and that for the weft the opposite, called "cross band" and "open band." It was a nice point to spin the exact amount for a web without having a little left or being a little short—for one spinner would spin yarn that would yield more length to the skein than another, and it was common to have a little warp left or to be a little short, and have to spin to make out from the weft slubbing and mix it among the other. This caused the weaver some trouble in tying threads up, when they broke, to use the proper kind of twist, which if not warped into the web properly showed itself, and was a defect. Both warp and weft were often left, and from fear of the consequences if carried back to the manufacturer men were under some temptation to sell it or make away with it, while some would save it till short, and use it when practicable. From all these various causes, and many more which might be enumerated, it will be seen that making cloths uniform was next to impossible, and where merchants weighed the pieces, as well as measured not only the lengths but the widths as well, manufacturers at that day had much to contend with.

CHAPTER VIII

Burling and Burlers

"Moity" wools—Burling cloths—Great losses sustained—What
Burling is and who does it—Dark weather—A bad scour—A great
institution—Burlers know all, and *more*—Listen at a Burling-
house door—Slubbers and their business—Ill usage and poor pay
of piecers—Slubbers earn good wages, and most of them spend
them—Condensers supersede slubbing—Prejudice against them—
False prophecies—America ahead of England—Condensers hold
their own, and slubbing dies out.

Any remarks dealing with the manufacture of woollen cloths
would be deficient if nothing was said about Burlers and Burling.
Old manufacturers know what an important branch or department this was from 50, down even to 30, years ago. Large numbers of women and girls were burlers of cloth. Australian and
Cape wools were in course of time brought into general consumption, and these wools were in a bad condition compared with
what they are today, though with the present means of destroy-
ing vegetable matter in wools, and of taking out the old pests
of burrs and moits, it ceases to be such a nuisance as then. Fifty
years ago, there were many blues, blacks, browns, clarets, and
greens made, and every colour had various shades as well. After
they were sold in the balk, that is unfinished, by the manufacturer to the Leeds merchant, they were sent to the finisher,
who raised and cut them to gain a face on them, so that every
speck in the cloth was laid bare, and if the cloths were not clean
burled they were damaged or imperfect goods. All who are likely
to see our remarks will know what we mean by burling, and it is
therefore only necessary to say that when the cloth was scoured
so as to show all the burls (specks), a burler's business was to
pick them out with small irons, which had fine points, and could
be easily and rapidly closed so as to pull the specks out. During
dark weather, or if the cloth was not properly cleaned in the
scouring, it would probably prove burly, and much of the cloth
made was very bad to make free from burls. This department
often gave great trouble and anxiety to the manufacturer, lest
cloths should either not be properly done, or cost too much doing,
for thousands of pounds have been deducted from what manufacturers expected to realise owing to burly cloths. It was customary for the merchants to see how the cloths proved with

regard to burls before they paid for them, or to pay something
on account, stopping a balance till the goods were finished.

This burling was a great institution of itself, formerly. Scores
of women and young girls might be seen going to and fro fetching ends on their shoulders to burl, or taking them back when
done. Many manufacturers had burling houses or sheds, with
several boards or tables to work on; others put their burling out.
Some burlers hired burling sheds, and got work where they could;
while many burled in their own houses. There was much difference in burlers: some were quick, some slow, some reliable,
others not. All the burled ends of cloth had to be *pearked* to
see whether they were clean. Some would be only a few minutes
in passing satisfactorily, while others were always a long time,
having to be re-burled on the peark. It was amusing to listen
outside the burling house where a few boards of burlers were
at work. They know all that is passing in the village: what the
old courters are doing and saying; who have just begun the
business; who are intending to begin; who want but cannot succeed; who have broken off their engagements, and why; the
faults, if not the virtues, of all; what births have taken place;
what are going to take place; the christenings, weddings, and
deaths. They know people's circumstances; how much some owe
to the grocers; and what some wanted to owe, and how cour-
teously, or it might be roughly and rudely, they were prevented.
They know how persons were dressed last Sunday, and how they
will be dressed next; the latest styles and fashions, the cost of
nearly every bonnet, shawl, and dress. Then the burlers attend
various churches or chapels, and sometimes in passing a few
boards of burlers you would be apt to think there was either a
concert or some religious service going on. They know all the last
Whitsuntide school tunes, and most of the old substantial ones,
such as Luther's Hymn, etc. There is most exquisite harmony, and
not a mere rehearsal, for they are singing daily. If these burlers
had had a chance of a decent education, and had chosen to
follow it up, the burling shed might have been a kind of college,
for there was very little noise caused by their work; so that they
could converse freely, and did so. Unfortunately, there was much
tittle-tattle to be heard; backbiting and slander were too common. A burling house was something like an epitome of the
world, where the most virtuous had some faults, and the worst
had some redeeming qualities. But another distinct class were
males, not females—and were called

SLUBBERS

These drew out the cardings, and wound them onto coppings as
slubbing, ready for the spinners to spin on their jennies. Slubbers

could earn about twice as much as the hand-loom weavers could, but paid the little boys and girls who were piecers (rubbing the carding ends together) a very small pittance—only three shillings or three-and-sixpence for standing doing their work a whole week of sometimes ninety hours. Some of the slubbers behaved very badly to these young boys and girls, beating them most cruelly. In winter time fathers might be seen carrying their children on their backs by five o'clock in the morning through deep snow to their work at the mills. Many with crooked legs might be seen—the result of standing fifteen, and sometimes sixteen, hours a day piecing. Though these slubbers could earn such good wages, yet as a class they were considered a drunken people, and somewhat extravagant in other respects. Probably working long hours tended to lure them to drink and excitement when not working, especially on Saturday nights and Sundays, as one extreme often produces another. Our remarks about the spare and scanty diet of the hand-loom weavers will not apply to this class, except in cases where they wasted their wages by want of frugality. If a young woman was courted by a slubber, she was looked upon as being fortunate. But the slubbers as a class were rather self-conceited. They thought themselves much superior to hand-loom weavers, and refused at times to sit and drink with the latter in the taproom at the alehouse, and passed into the bar, where they drank spirits, or from a superior tap of ales. We remember, however, it being a common remark, that if a slubber fell short of funds towards the latter end of the week (as many of them frequently did), and wanted a loan till the wage day, he had to go to a hand-loom weaver for relief—his fellow slubbers not being able to supply him. In course of time a terrible change took place for these proud slubbers—a machine was introduced which made the system of slubbing on what was called the "billy" useless; it was called

THE CONDENSER

from which came continuous threads of something like slubbing. Most of those likely to notice our letters will know what a condenser is; it dispensed with the old carding machines and billies.

The threads from the condenser were wound onto spools as they came from the machine, and were then removed to a frame in front of a "mule," where the threads were spun into warp and weft as required. It must be understood that long before condensers were introduced, spinning on the mule was common, which superseded the old spinning jenny (slubbing being spun by the mules), so that very few jennies were in use, but both the slubber and the jenny spinner were now dispensed with. Dispensing with slubbing and slubbers was not all that was effected by condensers. In this new process the fibres of the wool were placed lengthwise, which caused the thread to be much stronger. About forty years ago, whilst in America, we saw the condensers for the first time, and in the United States we found them almost everywhere. Every woollen manufacturer of any note had them, and we only saw after much travelling one billy for slubbing, and that was where only custom work was done, that is where farmers sent their wool to be made into such fabrics as they wished. Billies were confined to those out-of-the-way places, mostly, we were told, on streams with water power and one set of machines. We made inquiries about the condensers as to where they came from, and were told from Belgium and other countries on the continent of Europe; but at the time we are referring to they were made in the States. On our return to England, we explained the condensers to manufacturers, and spoke highly of them, but were laughed at and told that they might do for America, where everything was in such a rude state, and where they did not understand their business; or, they might suit worsted goods, but would never do for woollens, because the chief object in carding would be defeated, as a full thread was wanted, and not the fibre put lengthwise; that condensing would spoil fine cloths, by making them hard; that the cloth would have no elasticity, and would break like cotton goods, etc. We told them that French and Belgian goods were all condensed, and were being bought in the United States in preference to the English goods; they having a much higher finish and being *twice or thrice as strong*. After a long period, a few condensers were introduced into Pudsey for warps, and then those conservative manufacturers said: "Well, they may do for warps, but never for wefts." After a while, they were used for wefts, and then it was said: "Well, they may do for all-wools, but never for short stuffs, such as mungo and shoddy." We were telling this recently to a first-rate scribbler and condenser, called an "overlooker." He laughed most heartily, and pointing to a blend before us which was being condensed, he asked: "How could this job be done at all without a condenser?" and added: "There is not a bit of pure wool in it, and no man on earth could card this blend so as to make good yarn!" On looking at the thread on the bobbin after it had been spun, we saw an even, smooth, and strong thread of weft.

This shows that the United States of America were long ahead of us in the principle of condensing. Of course, every slubber was certain that a condenser was an infamous imposition, and would never act or answer the purpose, and most heartily hoped it would prove so. There was a little difficulty at first owing to

the ignorance of those whose business it was to attend to them.
If there are any old slubbers still living, they will never forget
the era, or first introduction, of condensers, for they were glad to
sit in the taproom or anywhere else after that, with hand-loom
weavers. The time for their humiliation had come, and it was
pitiful to see some of the slubbers—who for some time persisted
in the assertion that condensers would soon all be "thrown out,"
and carding and slubbing re-adopted—hanging about in a sad
condition. Their voices soon got considerably weaker; their faith
in billies the same; and unheeded condensers went on and pros-
pered. Carding and slubbing are now things of the past. Some of
the slubbers were too proud to do anything but slub. Others
learned to weave on the hand-loom, and others did anything
they could. Machinery, when first introduced, is a very serious
matter to those whose labour is thereby displaced. It is during
the transition time that certain classes of labourers suffer, though
ultimately it is a great benefit to society and the working people
where the new machine is adopted and set to work. Before we
were acquainted with the principle of condensing, the strength
of the French and Belgian superfine cloths imported in America
seemed inexplicable. We had imported some fine English black
cloths, but they were not comparable for strength. After seeing
those (to us) new machines at work, and understanding the principle of them, the mystery was all cleared away and made patent
to every man of common sense.

AN OLD-TIME PUDSEYER ON "PROGRESS IN PUDSEY"

(To the Editor of the "Pudsey District Advertiser")

SIR—Until the age of twenty-seven, I was a resident in your
district, and from Pudsey my wife came. Many of my relatives
and friends reside there still, and from old-time associations and
present-time feelings, my interest in the district is both deep
and vivid. Judge of my delight, then, when I became acquainted
some months ago with the fact that a real live Liberal newspaper had begun to be issued there; that is, not a mere sheet of
local items, but one strong in the spirit of Radicalism. And
Radicalism, as I understand it, not only goes to the root of principle, but also makes the people masters of their own destiny,
and insists that all true life depends for its wholesomeness on
never-pausing progress. May your right-principled and ably-
conducted paper flourish, and diffuse amongst the large population of your district those principles which are alone the
guarantees of justice and prosperity to the people!

The first part of your paper which I always turn to, however, on receiving it, is "Progress in Pudsey during the last Sixty Years." In publishing this work from week to week you are doing much to help the present generation of young people to understand, and, if they have a right mind within them, to appreciate the improved conditions in which they exist compared to their fathers and grandfathers; and to rouse within them the determination to do what they can to help in making the world better still for those who come after them. You are also engaged in preserving precious facts relating to the district from that oblivion to which they were fast hastening, and furnishing the future historian with material for real history. Surely, sir, if it is the people who form the nation, their condition socially, industrially, morally, and religiously—what they do, suffer, enjoy, think and feel—is real history, far more than the story of a few who have borne titles and made laws, the benefit of which has been mostly for themselves.

I am sure that Mr. Lawson has earned the right to tell the story he is now doing so well in your columns, for in every department of life—religious, moral, educational, social, industrial—he has worked hard in helping on progress in your district. And when one reform has been gained he has not given up striving, thinking that all was achieved; as his instinctive interest in life seems to have been for reform, so the attainment of one good thing has only been a prophecy of something better still. For more than thirty years I have known him as the earnest advocate of temperance, of political rights for the people, of co-operation, of moral purity, and a fairer religious life. It must be a keen delight to him in his green old age to look back and note that his toil, along with that of many others, in spite of some seeming failure, and of our present state falling far short of what it ought to be, has accomplished so much, and made bright with hope what may be done in the future. I would suggest that when this work has run through your columns, that it may be published in book form, so that it may take upon itself that permanent shape which, of course, a weekly newspaper cannot give.

Yours most truly,

AN OLD-TIME PUDSEYER

Sale, Cheshire, February 22nd, 1886.

CHAPTER IX

Low State of Education

Few schools—Uneducated teachers—Writing and Arithmetic not thought necessary—Books scarce, poor, and dear; and why— A good reader of a newspaper thought to be "far-learned"—Sunday schools—Ignorant teachers—A sin to write on Sunday— Wages kept down by law—Dangerous to educate the people— Quill pens—Borrowing writing materials—The Blacksmith and Barber's shops—Last news, old news—General ignorance of foreign affairs—No libraries for the people—Books in the cottage —Scarcity of waste paper—Street news—The Railway wonder— Monopoly of education by the aristocracy and the wealthy— American Republic and Education—When the people of England got political power they educated themselves—False Statistics by the Voluntaryists—What one did for himself—Exceptions no guide—Brutal punishment in weekday and Sunday schools— Ignorance breeds superstition.

With the foregoing general remarks on woollen manufactures, we will pass on to some other matters, and return to the subject in a future letter.

Young people ought to feel interested in a brief sketch of the state of education in Pudsey, fifty or sixty years ago. In this case we would have it understood that most of our remarks will apply to other villages, and most of the towns as well, at that time, with some exceptions where villages were favoured by free schools.

There were very few schools, and many of the teachers could not have passed our present Board Schools' sixth standard. Some taught nothing but reading and spelling, or knitting and sewing; others only reading and writing from printed copies (not being able to write themselves so well). A few taught arithmetic as well, but a grammar, geography, or history were scarcely ever seen in a school in those days. A few of the sons of the middle class learnt writing and arithmetic, but very few others learnt anything but reading. Large numbers never entered the door of a schoolhouse—having to work at something when they arrived at school age, or were allowed to run about all day, as if they were mere animals, and not capable of cultivation, or did not possess faculties waiting for, and needing, development. Writing was looked upon by many parents as a mere luxury for the rich only, and never likely to be wanted by their sons and daughters. A person who was a good reader of the newspaper, and could talk about various wars, battles, and sieges, was looked up to by the people, and said to be a "great scholar" and "a far-learned man." There were few school books, and those were of a poor kind—the tax or duty on paper, and the small demand, causing them to be very high in price. Sunday schools were in their infancy, and there was considerable prejudice against them at first, especially if writing was taught. Many of the teachers were very unfit for their position, and knew less than some of their pupils, and were appointed as teachers because older than the rest. Besides, the great or prime object of Sunday schools with many was not so much to teach children to read, as to make the school a kind of nursery which should supply the church or chapel with ad-herents to its particular faith or creed, and thus replenish it by adding to the church membership. It was quite common for some of the little ones when they returned from Sunday school to talk to their parents about the many errors of the teachers; but even that state of things was better than having no school. Very few attempted to teach writing in a Sunday school—that being looked upon as a desecration of the Sabbath. The aristo-cracy, who were the only lawmakers in this country, and who were thought to be far more wise than the common tradesmen and commercial classes, never made the least attempt to educate the people. On the contrary, they did all they could to discourage it, by taxing all the necessaries of life. Very little could be pur-chased with what was earned as wages, which were kept down by law—for there are more ways of lowering wages than by directly reducing them, viz., by raising the price of what the working people purchase, which is called "reducing their pur-chasing power." Long since the time of which we are speaking, it was said how dangerous it would be to educate the people, and if the meaning was that an educated and enlightened people would not submit to be taxed and mis-governed by a select class of men having no sympathy with the masses, then the self-appointed rulers were right in their fears, as after events proved; but though dangerous to the aristocratic usurpation, it was favourable to the people's welfare. Not only was the people's food heavily taxed, which caused the poor to have plenty to do to get enough bread, but paper was taxed, and newspapers had a stamp duty of fourpence each to pay. There were no steel pens, only quill pens, and very few knew how to make a good pen from a quill. A very good sharp knife was required, which few were able to buy, as well as great skill, in making a good pen from a quill, and mending it when out of repair. There were no self-sealing envelopes as now, but sealing wax, and after that, wafers. Then, postage was too high for the masses to pay, had they been able to write letters, costing, as before said, a half-day's wage sometimes. Many people might be heard wishing for a letter from some absent dear one, while adding that they did not know how they could raise the money to pay for it when it did come. Hence it was common to see the working people going from door to door, trying to borrow the postage on the arrival of a letter. Those who could write a little had often to go about borrowing materials to write a letter with; and one or two in a neighbourhood wrote the letters for the rest.

Newspapers were scarce and dear; very few could read them. There was a blacksmith's shop where several met to hear and read the newspaper, subscribed for amongst them weekly, and costing twenty times as much as the same matter would cost now. One of them read for the rest, and explained. He was looked upon as a very learned man, and so he was for the times in which he lived. There was one slight drawback, viz., he had considerable self-conceit, and thought he knew more than he really did, though very few of the many blunders he made were ever detected in those days, and if he was contradicted by any other knowing one, who might happen to drop in during the readings or conversations, his old pupils mostly voted him in the right. After all, this reader and expounder of the newspaper, from fifty to sixty years ago, was far ahead of the bulk of the middle class at that time, though he made many serious blunders, as we have said, not on mere matters of opinion, but on matters of fact, relating to history and geography. Others, who had a desire to know what was going on in the world, went to the inns, where a weekly paper was taken in, and where someone would read for the company. A barber's shop, where people went once each week to get a shave, was a kind of rendezvous for that day's literature. We said barber's shop, but the man did not make a living by shaving alone. He worked at some other business during the remainder of the week, and was a barber on Saturday. At that time it gave a kind of authenticity to any rumour to say: "I heard it at such an one's, where I went to be shaved." As for hair-cutting, people mostly cut each other's.

There were no railways, telegraphs, or ocean steamers; so that the news received from foreign countries might be three or six months old. If the news referred to the action of British forces—to battles and sieges—great changes might have taken place, reverses, defeats, or victories, since the last news left the scene of engagement. Even home news, that from some of the most extreme parts of the United Kingdom, would be so long before being received, that the latest news would now be called old, and almost forgotten. The high price of newspapers, and the fact that there were so few able to read them, made their circulation so small that the proprietors could not afford to have a large staff of reporters and correspondents in every part of the world (as some have now) to give something like a correct account of what took place. Hence the news was generally less reliable than now, especially such as came from the seat of war, where it had been purposely falsified to gain some special object for the time being. This was particularly the case in our dealings with the United States of America, not only long before the time of which we are speaking, but long after.

There were no libraries for the people, who had no access even to the few books there were; and the house that had a family Bible, hymn-book, prayer-book, or catechism, the Pilgrim's Progress, or News from the Invisible World, together with a sheet almanack nailed against the wall, was considered well furnished with literature. Others would be content with a sheet of Christmas hymns, sheet songs, and a number of the "last dying words and confessions" of culprits hung at York; or perhaps some little books on such matters as "Jack and His Eleven Brothers," "Jack and the Beanstalk," "Little Cock Robin," &c. A house that had a sampler done by one of the family framed and hung up, was considered a somewhat superior house for a working man—even if the needlework was not done to perfection. There was not as much waste paper thrown or blown about as we see now. No, waste paper meant something then, and was not as now—almost given away.

One great institution relied upon very much in those days, was "street news"—men shouting or singing news through the village. As already mentioned, the hanging of a murderer, got up in a sensational way, and frequently written before the event took place, as facts proved, was a great attraction. The inhabitants would stand at their doors and listen, or crowd around the man with amazement. Much of the news, true and false, was circulated in this way. We remember the sensation caused by one of these street vendors of news when the railway between Manchester and Liverpool was opened. The man sang a rude rhyme through the village, and we remember still the words:—

"Manchester and Liverpool they are two funny places,
Coaches are running every day without any horses," etc.

Most of the spectators had doubts about the possibility of its

being true. Some said it was a "lie," and when the great statesman—Huskisson—was killed by a train on the occasion, whilst
shaking hands with the Duke of Wellington, fifty-five years ago,
the doubters and disbelievers in "running coaches without horses"
seemed to have proved they were right. It was said by many that
in travelling in such a way, one-half of all, at least, would never
ride a second time, and with the then utter ignorance of the
masses as to the principles of locomotion by steam on railways,
it was impossible for them to think otherwise than they did.
Even men from whom a better knowledge might have been expected had many doubts as to the success of railways; no wonder
then that the common people should have no faith in them.

We have already referred to those who had the exclusive power
to govern this country at this time, and who purposely kept the
people in ignorance as long as they could. They believed education to be a good thing for their own class, for they monopo-
lised the best schools and colleges. We may be thought intolerant
and uncharitable in this observation, but were this the proper
place we should prove it from their own statements. The people
of the United States of America from first winning their independence, united as one man to make ample provision for the education of all their sons and daughters, and ever since in every
new settlement land for schoolhouses, and for income as well,
is set apart; and where there is a school tax levied, no tax is
so willingly and cheerfully paid as it. Their action—the action
of people politically equal, having got rid of the British aristocracy—was to educate all its future citizens, as the best safeguard
of their union; and as soon as the people of England got the
least political power they did the same. The English aristocracy
not only taxed knowledge in every shape and form, but even
light for the body, in the shape of the window tax; probably
they loved darkness rather than light "because their deeds were
evil." If it were possible to picture the low state of education in
Pudsey from fifty to sixty years ago, and present it to the young
people of today, it would seem to them incredible. Let us not be
misunderstood: It was not Pudsey alone; the surrounding villages
were in the same condition of dense ignorance except in some
isolated cases where a free school might be, or one assisted by
endowments, and hitherto not purloined by the rich. Such cases,
however, were rare, and the condition of the whole nation was
most deplorable. Even thirty years or more after that time, the
lamentable state of the people of this country as regards education was proved, in spite of all the compiled statistics of the
defenders of voluntaryism to the contrary, and was forced upon
the people. Hence Mr. Forster's Educational Bill, which in spite

of all its defects (and they are many) has already proved one of the greatest measures ever passed by the British Parliament, and what was proved impossible to accomplish by individual action, is now being done by the united effort of the nation. The people were powerless before, while the self-constituted legislators of old did not wish to do it.

In concluding this article, we may add that there were some few boys and young men who by desperate and untiring efforts made considerable headway in general knowledge in spite of the almost insurmountable difficulties. If they could do that with everything against them, what might they have done had they possessed the facilities young men and women are favoured with today? We remember a few who, nearly fifty years ago, agreed to meet at five o'clock in the morning till six, to read and converse on grammar, history, geography, and theology. They also met on certain nights during the week, and though they had not the best of books, made great progress. There was one great drawback at that time to a young man learning to speak the English language properly: he was often charged with "wanting to talk fine," and wishing to appear above others, by those who had no taste for rising above the multitude. We were well acquainted with one boy who, sixty years ago, before ever he went to any school would find all the capital letters in the Bible, and ask his mother what they were called, and in this way learnt the alphabet. He also learnt to read easy reading in this way, and the first time he went to the Sunday school he was advanced from the "reading made easy" to the spelling book, and in a few weeks to the "New Testament" class. He was not long before he was in the first, called the "Bible class," and in the absence of the regular teachers found himself acting as a substitute— teaching boys twice his own age. Having a natural shyness, he did not like his position as teacher, and we have known him often do a very foolish thing when a word was being spelt, or one to be pronounced, viz., to give the wrong answer when he knew the right one, being ashamed to go to the top of the class above so many boys older than himself. It should be kept in mind that the boy's rapid progress was not all attributable to Sunday schools, for during the weekdays, whenever he had a spare moment, he would be reading and asking his mother or someone else to explain. The same may be said about his learning to write. He had no pen, ink, or paper, nor even a slate. But with broken pieces of pots, pipes, or chalk, he would be seen trying to write (such letters as he had seen) on doorsteps, doorstones, and causeways. When about ten years of age, he had by long saving of the halfpennies he received for running errands and for reading the hardest chapter in the Bible, which was the tenth chapter of Nehemiah, succeeded in hoarding tenpence-halfpenny, which he invested by buying a slate and pencil. The day he got that slate, he felt to be the proudest of his life. It was everlasting pen and ink to him. He took care of all the old copybook leaves his mother got from the shop with her soap, etc., wrapped in, and would be scribbling on that slate late and soon; writing letters and little compositions, without anyone to tell him anything. He wrote a long time before he knew how to write the letters Q and Z, and went to several neighbours who could write a little to ask them how they were written. But they all differed a little in the style of making them; so he resolved upon a style of his own, borrowing a little perhaps from all. After that he went on splendidly, for he was a good speller of words by this time, and though he never wrote at school, he ultimately could write rapidly and read it as easy as print, though never a fine hand. Very little schooling was this boy allowed, and only to learn reading, for he had to do something to earn a little when very young, and his parents said that nothing could hinder him from learning faster at home than anyone they knew who went to school. In after years he made the same rapid progress in arithmetic and other branches. This boy never objected to going to school, because he wanted to be learning something. But when very young he told his mother he was certain he could learn more at home, because, except when reading, he was sitting still in a cramped and unhealthy position three-fourths or more of the school hours, either waiting his turn to read and spell, or for closing time. We often feel sorry about the way children were treated in old-time schools. There was so much cane, ferule, and physical punishment inflicted on boys who were not bad, but being full of energy and wanting to be free and to have some exercise, were kept there doing nothing and expected to be still and quiet, which was unnatural, and in some cases impossible. We have sometimes thought that a little activity, even if it entailed a good thrashing, was better than no exercise at all. The era of which we are speaking was famous for the "rod." No precept, perhaps, was more carefully observed than that of "spare the rod and spoil the child." We have seen such punishment inflicted both at day and Sunday schools that if inflicted now would get the attention of a policeman. One rather obstreperous boy in a Sunday school was once most cruelly treated. He was held, after being most unmercifully beaten, with his head downwards, by several of the male teachers, they standing on benches holding his feet upwards, all the scholars looking on to get the benefit. Then he was held by four teachers, each one having the boy by a hand or foot, face downwards for a long time. The scene now reminds one more of the old days of the Inquisition and tortures than a Sunday school. But we must stop, or we might write much more on the severe punishment at that day in schools. No wonder they should be looked upon as prison houses, and hated by those full of life and activity, for there was very little to make them attractive, or calculated to make children like to go to school.

The case of the self-taught boy referred to before, shows what can be done by "self-help," without which the best teachers and libraries are comparatively worthless. It would be foolish to expect all boys and girls having the same tastes and zeal for knowledge that he had, to stop up at nights after the fire was "raked," and the rest of the family had gone to bed, holding his book sometimes near the grate—his only light being what came from the few red cinders there—or perhaps he might be favoured by the light of a candle—poring over books and problems. The famous William Cobbett accomplished great things under somewhat similar difficulties, though we do not meet with a Cobbett once in a century. If this Pudsey boy had been favoured with such opportunities as boys and young men possess today, with his relish for books and learning, it is reasonable to conclude that he would have made a far superior man to what it was possible for him to be, after being reared as he was.

It is the duty of society to see that all its citizens are well educated; not merely for the sake of the individual, but for the sake of the well-being of the social compact itself. For, however the general spread of knowledge may endanger the interests of a class, it tends to secure what is of far more importance—the welfare of the toiling millions of wealth producers.

In our experience as Englishmen, we have had ample proof that Education when left to the voluntary efforts of parents is shockingly neglected. The bulk or majority of the working people find it so hard and difficult to get the necessaries of life, indispensable to existence, that they could not be expected to educate their children—entailing not only a heavy school fee, but the loss of labour their children might perform if not at school. Though the National or Board School system may cost a tolerable sum of money, yet when the quality of its teaching is taken into account, individual action could not do as much so cheaply. Better still, the school fees or tax are made to extend through life, and are therefore light during the time parents have their children young, and are not able to assist them in procuring food and clothing. We long for the time when education shall be free to all, so far as school fees go, since they have proved to be the greatest hindrance to school attendance. Whilst working people's children are at school, they are to feed and clothe, and the whole cost would be much easier to pay if spread over a lifetime in the shape of rates or taxes, than in school fees as now, paid in most cases whilst parents are least able to do so.

With the low state of education there was in Pudsey, from fifty to sixty years ago, it may readily be inferred that superstition in various forms would be widespread, and this subject we propose to deal with in our next letter.

CHAPTER X

"Superstition the Child of Ignorance"

Witchcraft believed in—Unbelievers in it called Infidels—Persons supposed to sell their souls to the devil—"Wise men" consulted—Virtue in a horse-shoe—Telling "Boggard Tales"—Children made unhappy—The "Padfoot," a ghost and the results—Favourite places for ghosts—Satan, his cloven-foot, and sulphur—Frightening children—Lucky and unlucky days, persons, and places—Boggards have a flourishing time of it—How to make boggards—Why are they scarcer?—Deaths, the result of bad sanitation, thought to be the will of Heaven—Sanitary science kills such notion.

In proportion as people are deprived of knowledge and are ignorant of the causes of what they constantly see and hear, their imagination is let loose, and, their reason being weak, they become a prey to every false rumour, or popular prejudice and delusion.

There was a time when a belief in witchcraft was almost universal. The law of England put to death all women and others supposed to be witches by drowning and burning, or inflicted tortures to extort confessions of guilt. Volumes might be written on this terrible mania, detailing the sufferings of innocent people. King James the First wrote a book in its defence; the greatest judges, legislators, and scholars spoke and wrote most eloquently to prove it. Ultimately, however, by the persistent labours of men of more philosophic minds, who dared to brave the obloquy, scorn, and hate of the times, being denounced as atheists and friends of the devil—by such men's influence the laws against supposed witches were abolished under George the Second. But the people had become so infatuated with the belief, that much of the superstition survived the abolition of the penal enactments; and long after that date most people still believed in witches and wizards, and pointed to the Bible for proof. Fifty and sixty years ago witches were not put to death, but a very general belief in witchcraft existed.

This was not confined to Pudsey people—it existed in other villages as well. But this fact does not make the former more free from the galling yoke of superstition which often disturbed their peace both by day and by night. If persons were very unfortunate, or had much sickness and death, some woman, known or unknown, was believed to have done it; or else it was some man—a wizard—who had made a bargain with, or, as it was said, had sold himself to the devil, and had power over those he wished. On the other hand, there were "wise men" and "wise women" who could tell such as were witched what to do, and how to punish the witch or wizard, and break the spell or charm; and it was quite common for such to go to them from Pudsey. One mode of keeping witches out of a house was to nail a horseshoe behind the house door, which we have often seen.

Such was the superstition at the time of which we speak, that the whole atmosphere was supposed to be full of good and bad spirits, on errands of mercy or of mischief; the latter mission always preponderating—the evil spirits mostly prevailing over the good.

Let us imagine ourselves in Pudsey as it was sixty, or even fifty years ago, on a dark and stormy winter's night, sitting by some fireside, with or without the dim light of a candle; a few neighbours—men, women, and children—sitting together. The children both dread and like to hear what are called "boggard tales." They ask the older people to tell them some tale they have heard before, or a new one. The pitch darkness outside, and the comparative darkness within, and the howling moaning winds, and perhaps heavy raindrops pattering against the window panes, cause everyone's imagination to be in full vigour, ready to drink in the weird stories. Every eye and ear is centred on the narrator. One tells of dreams he or she had before a certain death or deaths took place, which all came true; another remembers a dream about a wedding which proved to be a sign of a funeral in the family. Some have had the nightmare, which they call "bitch dowter" (probably the result of a deranged digestion), when they saw a woman they knew well, as fair as ever they saw anyone in their life, standing over them with a dagger or "whittle" (carving knife), threatening to murder them, whilst they could not stir hand or foot, being held spell-bound by this Pudsey woman, who was a witch, or at least had power from the devil to do mischief by her ill-wishes. They tell of ghosts they have seen, or that have been seen by someone they know, or knew; or else been seen by someone who told it to another well known by a friend of theirs. Then they tell of well-known ghosts that have visited well-known neighbourhoods from time immemorial, and been seen by scores of people, though they may not remember any single person who ever saw them; but it is well known by all, especially the old people. They tell of seeing the padfoot, or "guy tresh," the "white rabbit," of hearing the "night whistler," the "dead watch"; of heavy feet going up and down steps of chambers or cellars; or of hearing something like a pack of wool rolling about on chamber floors or steps; of hearing knocks, cracks, thumps, moans, groans, shrieks, or sighs and sobs, and all kinds of unearthly noises. The time arrives when many of them have to go home. Those who are timid dare not go alone after listening to the many doleful tales. The most courageous have to go with the others, whilst some stay till they are fetched by some of the family. They hurry along in the wind, rain, and darkness, hardly knowing how they get home; probably they see some object which in their morbid state of mind they could swear was a boggard of some sort. That night some of them dare not go to bed alone, or if compelled to go, wrap themselves overhead in the bedclothes, almost frightened to death. At last they doze off, and have horrible dreams, which are additional proof that some evil spirits have been influencing them through the night. Both young and old have their lives made miserable by these most horrible superstitions.

At this time all those who deny the existence of boggards are called infidels and atheists. The Bible even is referred to as a proof of the truth of witchcraft; also the great John Wesley's Journal, as well as what are considered every day facts of experience with regard to ghosts and apparitions. A large majority of all you talk to believe more or less in boggards of one sort or other.

One person we knew well, fifty-five years ago, was in the habit of seeing the "pad-foot" on almost any dark night, in all kinds of shapes, forms, and sizes, from a pack of wool, to a bull, bear, ass, calf, dog or rabbit. There was generally heard a rattling of chains, and in every form could be seen large eyes like tea saucers. If two persons were together, and one only could see and the other not, by taking hold of hands both saw it. This same young man got drunk at times, though in every other respect he was a decent, conscientious person, and very exceptional in his education, being a good reader, writer, and arithmetician for that time. As for drinking, it was not looked upon as being such an enormous crime then, especially in a young man. One dark night, as he came down Tyersal Lane, a woman walked beside him, having a white cap on, bound round with a black ribbon, and had on also a bedgown dress. He was convinced that it was his mother, who was a well-known Methodist at a time and place when being one meant much more than it does now; but she had died when this young man was only a few weeks old. This made such an impression on his mind that though not sober then, he was by the time he got home. He joined the Methodists, and afterwards became a local preacher. This affair was looked upon, both by the young man himself and others, not only as a direct interposition of Divine Providence, but as a proof of the existence of apparitions. There seems in this case to have been some utility in the superstition.

If a dog was seen to bark looking up in the air, or to howl, it was a sure sign of speedy death, either of persons in the neighbourhood or some of their relations.

There were local ghosts, and there were more cosmopolitan ghosts. All of them had been seen or heard either by persons then living or by truthful persons who, though dead, had told their experience to others.

There were several at Jumble's Well; also at Green Top, where it was said a parlour had a flagstone stained with blood, and though the flag had been taken up and replaced, the blood stain struck out in the new one. It was said that once upon a time a horrid murder had been committed there, and this stain was to be a perpetual sign. There were ghosts at Greenside, and haunted houses in Fartown. Ghosts in Bankhouse Lane, Bankhouse, and Bailey Gallows, and both children and many upgrown people would try not to pass those places in the dark, or increase their speed if they did, whilst their hearts beat louder. There were boggards at Littlemoor, Lowtown, and Boggard Lane; and about the old Chapel and the Church, after the dead were buried there, the locality near was believed to swarm. In fact, at that time spirits were either seen or expected to be seen whenever anyone's death occurred, and the neighbourhood for a time after was a terrible terror to many.

Satan, or the devil, was often seen in various forms on his errands of temptation and deception. He appeared to one man who was very devout; but this was at Drighlington, though often told at Pudsey by persons who lived at the former place at the time, and who knew the pious man. One day he was fretting about his clothes being so ragged, and wondering how he would be able to get new ones, as he found it hard to get sufficient food; when all at once a person with the appearance of a gentleman presented himself and offered him lots of gold. The poor man suspected his benefactor, and looking down at the gentleman's feet, saw that he had a "cloven foot," which it was said was caused when the devil was thrown out of heaven to the nether regions. The poor man immediately said, "Satan, I defy thee"; whereupon the gentleman instantly vanished, leaving a strong smell of sulphur behind, which was a certain proof of his identity. In whatever form Satan appeared, he had this cloven foot, and when he made his exit left a strong smell of brimstone behind him.

It was a common practice of parents when their little ones were naughty to tell them there was a black boggard up the chimney, or coming down to fetch them; also for them to make noises is secret, or knocks, said to be "Tom knocker," to intimate the presence of boggards; or to shut up their children in cellars and other dark places for the black boggards to take them. No one can tell the sufferings from fright experienced by thousands of little ones under the impression that they were going to be fetched by some ugly monster or malicious ghost. It is possible that some remnants of this worse than barbarous custom may still be practised by some parents; if so, they little know the dangerous effects and the demoralising influence of such, as it is a species of falsehood which their children, sooner or later, will discover, when less reliance will be placed on their parents' words, after finding out how they have been imposed upon by bogus boggards.

Then there were lucky and unlucky days, persons, places, actions, and dreams. It was thought to be a proof of future good luck for a man with dark hair to enter one's house first on Christmas or New Year's Day; and for any kind of man rather than a woman. Bad luck to take a light or allow one to be taken out during Christmas time. Bad luck to spill salt; and so it was when that article cost so much owing to the heavy tax on it. One of the most important articles in the literature of that day was a "dream book" explaining their meaning, and giving interpretations. There was no end to people's infatuation on the subject of dreams. To dream of fruit out of season meant grief out of reason, etc. Young women who ate the first egg of a pullet before going to bed would dream of their future husbands; and on Shrove Tuesday, called pancake day, young people would turn their pancake and run to the door to see their partners for life. Fortune telling was very common, and many still living can tell startling stories about what they were told by fortune tellers, or planet rulers, as astrologers were called, who described their future husbands just as well as if they had known them. Persons are now liable to be prosecuted for following such a profession.

If we consider the dense and widespread ignorance of the people in past times, together with the dark lampless streets and lanes, the very little light even in the houses, we may easily see what a flourishing time boggards would have; for objects not clearly seen would assume all kinds of shapes, in accordance with persons' disordered imaginations. A little lime on a wall, the top of a wall being uneven, would be a ghost. To people sitting in darkness round a low fire, listening to the wind outside, the least noise would sound louder. A moaning wind would sound to some as it did to the person with a bad conscience mentioned in Miss Brontë's "Wuthering Heights," when it was heard to say in a most plaintive and suppliant tone, "Let me in; Let me in."

We have known persons who were somewhat sceptical about ghosts and boggards detect some imposition, and find that a candle had been carried across the floor of a house, and had shone through the crevice of a window shutter, or door lockhole, and flitted to and fro in the street as the candle was moved, and this had been thought a genuine ghost. We have seen this effect produced frequently on a dark night. The fact is, people were generally too much afraid to examine and test the matter properly; they were so full of their infatuation that their imaginations coined boggards wholesale.

How is it then that there are fewer boggards now than sixty years ago? In the first place, knowledge has been spread abroad. Such men as Chambers have scattered cheap publications broadcast through the land. Their miscellaneous tracts were unequalled by anything in publishing ever known before. One we well remember on "Spectral Illusions" was just the right kind of thing to kill boggards and boggard tales, showing how people were liable to be mistaken and imposed upon—especially those whose vision was defective, etc. Then science generally made itself known, and even Professor Pepper's Ghost has helped to extinguish the last remnants of the superstition, for then it became impossible to distinguish the genuine from the manufactured. But above all, the cheapening of books, and especially of newspapers, by the abolition of the tax on paper and stamp duty. Still more than all perhaps by the introduction into the villages of gas for the houses and streets, so that people could see objects more clearly, and were not so easily deceived. Gas was stationary, and not moved about the house like a candle; so that mimic ghosts could not be made in the old fashion. In dark weather gas made it lighter than day. We remember when a certain person who had looms in his chamber first lighted up with gas—in mid-winter—the change from candles to gas was so surprising that he exclaimed, "No more day leet for me!"

We ourselves were always rather sceptical when a boy about some of the boggards, and had the boldness to make some of them out as being natural objects. We often asked how it was that they only came at night, when they could not be seen clearly. Some strong believers in ghosts seemed to be amazed at our exposing some of their favourite boggards, as if they had rather they had been real than spurious.

Another most serious and mischievous superstition, everywhere prevalent, was the belief that when any child died, it was the will of the Lord that it should be so. Sanitary science was at that time very little known or understood, and the few who had studied the matter and made themselves acquainted with the laws of life, health, and disease—who spoke of the possibility of preventing many of the deaths both of children and upgrown people—were called "Infidels." Now it is easy to see that so long as people had the idea that the mortality of a town or country was just what it was intended to be by Heaven, they would be apt to make less exertion to save life, lest they should be opposing the intentions of Providence. What do we see today? Strange, but most welcome difference. Our most orthodox papers and books, written by persons the most devout, talk about the large number of deaths annually which might be prevented, and which it is our duty to prevent. Officers of Health can tell us nearly the exact number of deaths that will take place under the present sanitary conditions and with the same habits of the people in the United Kingdom during the next twelve months. People still believe in Providence, but it is a more reliable one, more rational; one that can be depended upon—not fickle and variable, one thing today and another tomorrow, snatching a child here and another there without any apparent reason or cause. Providence now is seen to have fixed methods; so that by people studying its arrangements and conforming thereto, health, life, and happiness can be enjoyed.

Society is now influenced more by facts of art and science than dreams, random luck, tales of planet rulers, fortune tellers by palmistry, or a capricious Providence. Local Boards insist upon proper ventilation, drainage, and the avoidance of other disease breeding nuisances. The law now steps in and prevents people selling what they like, building such dwellings as they like, making the interest of the many of more importance than the whim or self-interest of the few. Property has now its duties as well as its rights.

And after all, sanitary science is in its infancy, scores of thousands of lives being sacrificed each year. Notwithstanding all the progress made during the last sixty years, which is incalculable, our children's grandchildren will probably wonder at our ignorance, with all our boasting. One thing is certain—that progress during the next fifty years will be greater than during the last hundred, having so many more facilities now than before to effect it.

CHAPTER XI

Manners, Customs, Sports and Pastimes

Barbarous manners and customs the result of ignorance—Pudsey no worse than other villages—Old-time clanships—Insulting strangers—"Pudsey blacks"—Pugilists visiting feasts—Young men standing in groups—Village constable—Indecent remarks to passers by—Alehouses and Chapels—Doing mischief—Teetotalers thought to be crazy—Alcohol indispensable at Sacrament—Prize fights—Dog and Cock fighting—"Cobbler Monday"—Christmas both merry and sad—Old-time Football and the new—Dancing single step—Easter and Fulneck Tide, etc.—The low state of Yeadon—Intercourse with other villagers destroys clanship—Cobden's French Treaty makes us fear the French less—Cricketing, old style and new—Cricket a civiliser—Cruelty to animals—Hate of the Irish—Children mob them—Old-time Alehouses—Chartism—A test of best ales—Drunk for sixpence—The sort of songs sung—The war spirit—Long working hours.

If the people of either a village or a country are denied the means of education and of gaining general knowledge—shut out from all great moralising and civilising influences—they cannot help being ignorant and superstitious, as well as rude and rough in their demeanour; so that their manners, customs, sports, and pastimes are sure to be what those who are better informed and more refined will consider somewhat savage and barbarous.

In what we may say about Pudsey as it was from fifty to sixty years ago, under the above heading, we wish it to be understood that it was not worse than most other surrounding villages were in proportion to their population; nor will our remarks apply to all its inhabitants, but to the prevailing element.

In the first place, narrow local prejudices, forming a kind of clanship, existed not only between the various villages, but in the same village. Hence in Pudsey there was a Sodom clan, a Fartown clan, and a Lowtown clan—the latter of which was probably the strongest—with minor clans in other parts of the village. It was often rather disagreeable for a person from one part of the village to pass groups of young men standing together in another part, as he was almost certain to be insulted by coarse threats, or else, worse still, to be roughly treated. Of course this sort of conduct was reciprocated, for the same young men had to meet similar treatment when they passed through the parts of the village where they did not reside.

In a milder form and on a smaller scale it was what takes place amongst the uncivilised races, where various tribes are constantly attacking each other. If a person, especially a young man, went to reside from one part of a village to another, he was looked upon as a kind of foreigner or interloper, who had no right there. We have known persons both insulted and assaulted for a long time till they got initiated or naturalised. The new-comer might be a spirited and courageous youth with plenty of pluck, and prepared to fight his way in self-defence; if so, he was much sooner respected than if inoffensive, non-resistant, and submissive. We have already noticed the narrow local prejudice in the matter of courtship by lads and lasses living in different parts of the village.

Pudsey has often been charged with pelting and otherwise insulting strangers, and the only fault we have to find is in the charge being made as if it applied to the people in recent times. At the time we are speaking of it was too common not only in Pudsey, but in most of the surrounding villages as well.

Again, the people of Pudsey have often been called

"PUDSEY BLACKS"

But however true this may have been in times far back as regards character, when applicable to all populous villages, it has long since ceased to have any special application to Pudsey. Taking into account its population fifty or sixty years ago, even then it was no more rude and rough in its character than other places. No doubt it would have more rough characters, but it had twice or thrice as many inhabitants as most other villages, and could afford to have more roughness, so to speak, and yet not have a larger percentage of it than its neighbours. Some hold that "Blacks" did not refer to their character, but to their blue smocks and coloured faces made by their labour.

We have spoken of clanship in Pudsey itself, but every village at that day formed a clan against other villages. Whatever petty prejudices existed intrinsically, when villagers met each other at the various feasts or at other gatherings, the various Pudsey clans would combine against outsiders, and being, as a rule, larger in numbers, would generally be the victors, and therefore would be likely to get the reputation of being worse than others, and deserve the appellation of "Pudsey Blacks," which possibly had a double application. The Pudseyites were a bold and sturdy lot, and being more numerous than others were, would not be so easy to conquer by rude physical force, though we remember a case where they were overpowered by numbers, and many nearly killed, one being killed outright.

It was customary for the pugilists of all the villages to visit each other's feasts, and in many cases with the avowed object of meeting other pugilists there. It was quite common to see several rings formed, in which men stripped to their bare skin would fight sometimes by the hour together, till the combatants were not recognisable, being so deformed by wounds and besmeared with blood and dirt. Out of one fight others would arise, and both on the Sunday and other feast days nearly one-half of the time engagements of this kind were going on in one or other parts of the village in smaller or larger affrays. Most of them took place during the after part of the day, when the men were maddened by drink, and having had time to get excited by boasting of what they could do with each other.

Even in Pudsey, not at feast time only, but on Saturday nights and on Mondays as well (called Cobbler Monday, as cobblers seldom worked on that day), men might often be seen fighting till almost exhausted, and sometimes even women might be seen helping to form the rings, and shouting encouraging words to the combatants. There were no policemen in those days; nothing but village constables, whom the crowd would prevent from interfering, or it might be the constable would allow them to have a few rounds more, especially if he saw the fight was likely to end soon; while at other times when told at his own house that a fight was going on, he would say: "Never heed them; they get their wages as they go on." Many at that time kept dogs for fighting, and frequently two dogs might be seen fighting on the highways in the village till both animals were nearly dead. There were great "dog battles," as they were called, for wagers, and no one interfered. Gamecocks were also bred and trained to fight with steel heels put on, when one was almost certain to be killed. Others were kept by some of those who kept hens, to fight for what they called the "walk." You could not have gone through Pudsey at that day without seeing many of them with swollen heads, perhaps blind altogether of one eye, or "blanked" as they called it. In many cases we have known one of the cocks to be killed in the fight. Yes, we have known much money spent, and ill-feeling amongst neighbours engendered, in fighting cocks for the "walk."

What was called the prize ring was very popular. Men were kept on purpose as pugilists, and fought each other for wagers. Some of the fights came off in Pudsey and the neighbourhood. We remember seeing one on Baildon Moor (a favourite place for such), and large numbers went from Pudsey to see it. These were professional pugilists, and fought more than two hours, till it was with difficulty that one could be distinguished from the other, so swollen, blackened, and disfigured were they.

Then it was common for young men to stand in groups at certain places and lane ends, or near stiles on footpaths, playing at pitch and toss, or talking of the next feast or holiday, or the frolics of the last; singing sometimes indelicate songs, whistling and dancing single step, jumping, boxing, or wrestling; and, worse still, in making audible personal remarks about single or married women who might pass—conduct which today would send the perpetrator to prison. There were innocent sports, for pastime, such as playing at "taws," in which some were noted players, peg top spinning, and knur and spell; while the girls would skip with the rope, or play with the ball or shuttlecock. "Duck nop," or knob, was a great game with young men, but it was rather dangerous. A little stone was placed on a larger one. The business of one of the players was to put the little one on when knocked off by any of the other players, who threw stones at it. If any person was touched by the tender in fetching back his stone, he had to be the tender. But the little stone must always be on the big one when a person was touched, and he must always have the stone he threw in his hand when touched, or else have touched it.

The Rugby Rules in playing football appear to us objectionable. But you should have seen football in Pudsey fifty or sixty years ago. Down-towners playing up-towners; in wet weather, bad roads, and played through the village; breaking windows, striking bystanders, the ball driven into houses; and such "shinning," as they called kicking each other's legs. It was quite common to see these up- and down-towners kicking each other's shins when the ball was a hundred yards away. Of course, many received serious injuries. There were dancing matches for wagers, and publicans offered prizes for the best dancer of single step: there were many good dancers of single step in Pudsey and the villages adjoining.

We have no right to look down with scorn on these old-time Pudsey folks. They were what their surroundings had made them. Most of those who could afford it went to the ale-house, and many, as now, went who could not afford it. But at that time there were only two places to go to in spending spare time away from one's own house—the church or chapel, and the alehouse; the former were seldom open, while the latter was seldom closed. The first was not attractive, as we shall show in our next article, the second was made what was thought at that day attractive

for young men, and old men too, especially the former, full of
health, life, and vigour, who were shut up within narrow limits,
confined to the monotony of daily toil, kept in ignorance, and
who are to be pitied more than blamed. It is an open question
as to whether even a little active mischief was not better than
sitting still poring over their narrow surroundings. They certainly
thought so, and hence they kicked people's doors on dark nights,
to have a race with the inmates; put a slate on the top of chim-
neys to prevent the escape of smoke; and called people "nick-
names" to have them running after them. We remember a
number of young men one Saturday night (the great night for
frolic and drinking) taking a number of nearly new gates from
one neighbouring farm and hanging them on another close by
which needed them badly. On the Sunday morning there was
such laughing by the party who got the gates, and such threatening by the man who had lost them. All these little mischiefs were
done for fun, or for a "lark," as it was called, the perpetrators
having little or nothing better to do, and not from any malice
or ill-will to anyone. Had the young people of today no better
opportunities than they had, they would be no better than they
were.

We may remark here that Christmas was both a merry and yet
a sad time—there being so much drunkenness. We should not
wonder if some heathen visiting Pudsey on Christmas Day had
asked if their Christ lived and died a drunkard, that made them
honour His birthday in such a way. It would take too long to
go into particulars as to the way in which it was spent, except
that singing was common, and bands of boys, and, later in the
day, girls, went from door to door crying: "Pray yah nah Christmas box," or "Christmas drink." Whitsuntide was a great holiday,
but not as now, as Sunday schools were not so common. It is
these schools that have given that holiday popularity. But even
at that time this annual feast was talked about and looked forward to with great pleasure. There were such attractions in the
music, singing, walking through the village in fine clothes, and
after all to have a currant cake each, and as much tea as one
liked. Then there was the Easter holiday. Easter Sunday was a
great affair for Pudsey folks, owing to its being Fulneck Tide.
We have seen Fulneck crowded with visitors on that day, there
being splendid music at the Moravian Chapel; and many believed
that the dead could be seen to rise in the burial ground on Easter
Sunday morning. There was the Fulneck Inn in the centre of the
settlement, and there was much drunkenness indulged in by
visitors, to the great annoyance of the settlers. Ultimately, we
believe the sale of ale and spirits was given up, and the Inn kept

on as one of the real older-time sort for rational refreshments only.

Keeping in mind all that has already been stated about the low state of education—few schools, the bulk of them poor ones, few going to school at all, of course not many readers, and fewer still who could write; newspapers scarce and dear, books the same; no teetotal societies, and nearly all believing intoxicating drinks to be essential; no Mechanics' Institutes, or circulating libraries for the people—how then can we wonder if the people were not equal to those of our day in their manners and customs?

When Teetotalism first came up, the few who happened to be its first adherents and propagators were mostly persons of somewhat pale countenance, and the great proof of health at that day was ruddy complexion and robustness. We really thought they were carrying the thing too far, and that their self-sacrifice was endangering their lives. Teetotal advocates at first had no idea that alcohol in all forms was bad. But they thought that touching intoxicating drinks was dangerous, that total abstainers could never become drunkards, that they could manage to live without those drinks, and if their example were the means of saving a drunkard or preventing a person from being made one, it was well worth any sacrifice they made. No one that we are aware of at first thought it would be proper to take the sacrament without intoxicating wine. The whole community was looking on expecting that the first teetotallers would not long be able to survive, whereas there are one or two we know of still living after all these years of abstinence, and who lived to see the whole tone and conviction of society undergo a great change on this subject. Millions since then have proved that they could live and enjoy healthy and happy lives without intoxicating drinks, and even many of the ablest doctors have long since ridiculed the notion that those drinks are essential to health, while a large number say that they are not necessary even as medicine. In fact it has long since become a question with the public as to whether it is proper to allow the public sale of such drinks, and before long it is certain to be at the option of the people in a district as to whether they will have the alehouse or not.

Pudsey, we have always maintained, however low in intelligence and morals was equal to other villages.

It was our lot to work and reside at Rawdon and Yeadon for about six months, some fifty years ago, and we had every opportunity of seeing Yeadon as it was at that time. It was a common remark, made both at Rawdon and Yeadon then, that "Yeadon was the last place God made, and that He made it out of the refuse,"—or what we should now call "shoddy."

However bad Pudsey might be at that time, Yeadon was much worse, and had a larger number of reckless and low characters in proportion to its population. Very little work was done on Mondays, and public-houses were generally crowded with drunken men, pugilists and their backers. Very little work was done from Saturday to Tuesday by a large number. Prize fights and local fights for the championship were the chief topics of conversation. A pugilist once came to work there from Stanningley near Pudsey, and one night after one of the Yeadon champions had gone to bed, his backers waked him up to fight the newcomer. He got up and dressed himself, but soon found he was "nowhere" against the new pugilist, who drove him here and there and knocked him about just as he liked.

There is only one thing that we are aware of that may be said in favour of Yeadon's low state at the time (if such can be called in favour), which is this: more money could be earned there, and there were greater temptations to spend than at Pudsey. For in addition to superfine cloths, or at least a better kind of cloths, made by Thompsons and a few more, fancy spotted shawls were made as well. The reason why we have mentioned Yeadon in this connection is, because during the recent formation of Parliamentary Divisions under the Reform Bills, it was at first arranged that Yeadon should form part of the Pudsey Division. To our surprise, some inhabitants of the former place objected, and had very much to say as to what a disgrace it would be to belong to the Pudsey Division. We do not know that many who lived at or knew Yeadon fifty years ago, talked in this foolish way. We hope for their credit's sake they were younger people who were misled, and judged Pudsey from what it was in olden times, as reported to them by older people, and compared Yeadon as it was in 1885, which would be very unfair. We were sorry to hear that one gentleman when asked for proof that Pudsey was unworthy of Yeadon, or of being the centre of the Division, had nothing better to say than "Go to Pudsey!"—an old phrase with some who know very little of that place as it is today. This gentleman is one we have great respect for, a man in other respects possessing a large share of intelligence and sound common sense, but who after all had not been able to steer clear of the petty clanships and local prejudices which existed long before he was born. From our own knowledge, and not mere opinion, of Pudsey and Yeadon, had there been any valid objection to the political union, that objection might with greater reason have come from Pudsey—judging from their comparative characters fifty years ago.

But what folly there would be in judging either place from what it was at that time! Why a person who had lived at either one or the other so far back, and never heard of them since, on coming back would not believe the people were the descendants of the former inhabitants—so much are they both changed in their habits, manners, and customs, and in everything which makes up civilization.

There is no difficulty in accounting for the narrow prejudices and clanships in olden times. There was less intercourse, the chief means of travelling being by walking—except that the old people, or a few of the weaker sex, would ride with the common carrier to Leeds and Bradford sometimes. Less people see and know of each other, as a rule, and more jealous they will be of each other. Hence apart from the economical bearings of Free Trade, it is one of the best civilisers and preventatives of War. Previous to the great statesman, Richard Cobden, negotiating the Treaty with France, it was the common talk what a dangerous people the French were, and that they might be coming to invade and take England any day; and those who object to the Channel Tunnel being made belong to the old barbarous dispensation. What millions of money this constant bugbear of a French invasion has cost the people of this country! On the other hand, no doubt the French would be equally jealous of England, and a very little matter would have created war. But when the interests of the two countries were linked together and made mutual by frequent commercial intercourse, all this, or much of it, died away. More we know of a people, more trade we have with them, and a greater probability there is of peace being maintained. The greatest travellers, those who see most of the various races, peoples, and countries, are generally the freest from petty local prejudices. They come in contact with peoples having all kinds of notions, creeds, and customs, all equally honest and sincere. One who sees all this has his own little knots of narrowness unavoidably removed. Even the cheap excursions by railroads, of which many of the working classes avail themselves, and by which other localities are so easily reached, tend to liberalise the people's minds.

We remember the time when Cricketing was unknown in Pudsey, except as played mostly in the lanes or small openings in the village—with a tub leg for a bat, made smaller at one end for a handle, a wall cape, or some large stone, set on end for a stump (called a "hob"), and a pot taw or some hard substance covered with listing and sometimes sewed on the top with twine or band. They were all one-ball overs if double wicket was played; no umpires, and often those who cheated the hardest won. But see now to what perfection that game has attained! It was some time before the new style of cricket was played with the order and decorum we see today. When it first came into vogue village clanship was rather rife. Money was mostly played for, and frequent uproar, confusion, and even fighting took place, though the strict rules helped to curb all this very much—otherwise cricket between the different local clubs would have been impossible. Playing for money was ultimately given up, and looked upon as being low and degrading to the game. The winning club mostly got a new ball, and the various towns and villages continued to contend against each other for the mastery. As years have passed on, the behaviour of both players and spectators (especially the former) has become comparatively orderly. It is not uncommon now for the people of Pudsey to be seen applauding their opponents by clapping hands and by other marks of approval, when a good point is made in the shape of either hitting, bowling, fielding, or wicket-keeping. All this is as it should be, though very different to what one saw even thirty years ago. Cricketing has had a most wonderful influence for good on the young men of Pudsey—not only on the players, but on the spectators as well. By cricket, players are taught patience, endurance, precision, and courage. They are taught self-respect and gentlemanly conduct in bowing to the decision of the umpires, and derive physical benefit as well. The discipline taught by the game of cricket is great and invaluable, and we wish it every success.

Dumb animals were formerly much more cruelly treated in Pudsey than at present. Both horses and donkeys were worked in a most horrid and pitiful state, having such wounds and sores; and in old age, when unfit for work, they might be seen lame and hobbling along ready to drop with exhaustion—as was quite common for them to do, and die on the spot. Dogs were also badly used, having tin cans or other weights tied to their tails, then let loose, to run home almost mad with terror. Cats, too, were often worried by dogs being set on them, for mere dog practice, or for sport; and were hung, drowned, shot, stoned to death, thrown into wells, or buried alive.

Prejudice against the Irish is far from being dead yet, but at the time we are speaking of, if any came into the village gathering rags and bones or hawking small wares, they were often badly treated by the boys, while the older portion would look on and connive at it. They were mobbed with sods, etc., and all kinds of bad and threatening language was used to them. The lads were only carrying out in practice the spirit of their parents. They would shout various epithets to exasperate "Paddy," asking which way the bull ran, etc. You could scarcely hear a good word uttered in favour of the Irish. The people were saturated with the spirit of hate engendered by centuries of British misrule and oppression in Ireland. If a man employed an Irishman, he was looked upon by many as a kind of traitor to his country. Much of this feeling has died out, and the remainder will expire (except such bitterness as may be caused by difference of religion) when complete justice has been done to that unhappy country; for just in proportion as we have in recent years removed Irish grievances, to that extent have the English treated the Irish with respect.

The ale-house in Pudsey was once a better index of the manners, customs, sports, and pastimes, than now—because nearly all the male population went there, more or less. People went there because they had nowhere else to go for society. Whatever took place then came off at the ale-house, and there were not the many other attractions there are today outside the public-house. There were no political clubs and reading rooms, because very few had any political power, and therefore took very little interest in political matters. When CHARTISM was introduced a few of the most thoughtful talked about the rights and wrongs of the people, and denounced the aristocracy. But many of these men were strong believers in ale, and in having a fair share of it, and most of their meetings were at a publichouse. Certainly it would have been difficult for them to have met anywhere else at that time, except in the open-air, which was not always allowed, for it was not long before that time that an infuriated soldiery had cut and stabbed innocent men, women, and children, at the Peterloo massacre, in Manchester, when met peaceably. With all the defects of Chartism, there is reason to believe that Pudsey, had it not been for that agitation, would not now have been so Liberal in politics as it is today, but Truth never dies.

The conversation and amusements at the alehouse were all in accord with what we have said of the people of that day. Many who went had very little money with them, and most of them could have used what they spent there more profitably at home, in better ways; but they did not see things in that light. They looked upon intoxication as real strength and nourishment, and therefore mostly aimed at that alehouse where with the least money they could get well drunk. To prove a certain ale was cheap, and a good bargain they would say: "*I nobbut gat a quaart of Timothy, an I never knew ah I gat home!*" This ale, which had a great reputation for making people drunk, we believe was threepence for a pint, but then for sixpence a man could get insensibly drunk, and was considered a "cheap drunk." At the alehouse, besides talking about the gossip of the village, spinning long yarns of various sorts, cracking jokes, etc., they would play at dominoes, "shuvving the penny," "marrowing each other's coins," or "odd man-ing," and at puff and dart; or, if during the day, they might play at brasses, quoits, and skittles—all for ale. Or they would be singing songs, all joining in the chorus when there was one, or in the last two lines, if no chorus. The songs were like the times and the people, as they generally are; mostly on love, drink, and war. Some would now be considered indelicate and obscene, which were not thought so at that time. It would take up too much space, or we would give a list of those songs popular from fifty to sixty years ago in Pudsey. The war songs always made England "beat all creation," as the Americans say, both by land and sea. We suppose it was just the same in every other country, or there would have been fewer wars. The English lasses, as a matter of course, were at the head of all others, because they had seldom (if ever) seen any else to compare with them, and it was quite right that they should think (as is the case in all countries), most of those they knew most about. Some of the songs told them it was the finest thing in the world to get drunk, and we dare say it is not unpleasant getting drunk, but as a man used to say, *"It was nice getting drunk, but unpleasant getting sober."* At that day they had no idea that "those who made the quarrels" between nations "should be the only men to fight." Oh, no! they were ready both to fight and pay for all the wars their political masters brought about, by their quarrels, from petty spite, or to get honours, medals, places and pensions, at the people's expense. Then all "beverages" were spent at the alehouse, that is money paid when a person had a new suit on, and all "footings" money paid by a man when he came to work at a fresh place. Also "wake" suppers, when people began to work by candle or lamp light; as well as "slecking out" suppers, when in March they gave up lighting.

So long as human beings are deprived of innocent recreations and amusements, they will have recourse to such as are mischievous and degrading. People working at monotonous toil such long hours as they did, when they had work, would need relaxation. Young people of Pudsey today have a great variety of means of spending their spare time, not only innocently but beneficially, both mentally, morally, and physically; they had not then, and therefore it would be wrong to judge our forefathers by the standard of today. But much more remains to be done. The hours of labour each day made a total of 300 days a year for our forefathers, while our working days, working the same hours they did, would only amount to 200 days a year; in other words, we work about one-third less time than they did, and therefore have all that more time than they had for self-culture and innocent amusement. But, as we have said before, there remains still much more to do. More parks, gardens, and swimming baths; high-class schools, in which to study art, designing, etc., for the future progress and success of the people of Pudsey and the benefit of all around; gymnasiums for the physical development of both girls and boys; more music, and dancing, to give graceful action; more English grammar; more of everything tending to cheer the spirits in a rational way, and develop the faculties mentally, morally, and physically.

———

In this letter we do not pretend to have noticed all the manners and customs of Pudsey people in olden times, but a few only—sufficient to give young people a general idea; and before we deal with Theological Progress it may not be out of place to refer to a custom we remember to have frequently witnessed, called "Riding the Steng" (stang). If a man ill-used his wife, or a woman was thought to be very bad, the people in the neighbourhood would dress up an effigy of a man or a woman, as the case might be, made of straw, putting clothes on it so as to make it represent the criminal they wished to expose, which was then carried about the neighbourhood, amid shouting, hooting, and constant insult being done to it; after which it would be set on fire, and burnt to ashes. This "Riding the Steng" was much dreaded by people, whose outrageous conduct was probably thereby considerably curbed. This custom had very likely arisen from the once practice of burning witches and other culprits at the stake, and came as near "Lynching" as the law would allow.

A word or two may be said about the Pudsey dialect, which has much improved within our knowledge; we mean that a much larger proportion of the inhabitants speak better English. If people are not taught English they cannot be expected to speak it. When there was no, or very little, education, dialect would be the only thing known. But now that we have a system of National Compulsory Education in addition to the Mechanics' Institutes and Mutual Improvement Societies, in a few generations the dialect of Pudsey will be less known. Every county almost has its peculiar dialect, and even the Cocknies, but all these will in time be obliterated, though but slowly. It would be easy to show that many of the words used in the Yorkshire dialect were once good words and proper, but the English language itself as spoken and written (especially the latter) a hundred years ago, is not easy to read today, as it is continually changing.

CHAPTER XII
Theological Progress

An ignorant, superstitious, and rude people will have a
Theology to match—Terror to check vice—The chapel and the
ale-house—Church and Dissent—Church-rates—Bad feeling
caused—Political immorality—The old theology had no present
utility—Learning despised—Wise above what was written—
Science called "wordly wisdom"—Ignorance of the Bible—Praying
to reconcile contradictions—The State Church no criterion—
Great change in theology—Chapels more inviting—A pattern
Methodist—No whistling on Sundays—Religious football players,
cricketers, and harriers—Methodists and temperance—Ministers
more liberty—More charity towards sinners—A Methodist's
address to students—A good sign—The Owenites—Joseph Barker
—Hearing him preach—Barker's expulsion for heresy—Split in
the Methodist New Connexion—Trotter and Smith—Barker's
great labours—He becomes more heretical—Gets a steam printing press—Publishes the *People*—The Barkerites—Barker goes to
America—Returns an Agnostic—A co-editor of the *National Reformer* with Bradlaugh—The latter made sole editor—Barker
ends where he began—His death bed—Confession—Unitarians—
Science and other agencies liberalise the old theology.

In what we may say on this subject, we have no desire to wound
anyone's feelings. We are not writing in the interest of any
religious sect or creed, and shall simply aim at stating facts as
they have come under our own observation.

An ignorant people will be superstitious—have a low moral
standard—with a theology to match the same. It is impossible
for those who are badly informed to have an enlightened, liberal,
and rational theology. Some tell us it is best so; because that
religious terror if false is better than no restraint at all where
the people are ignorant of science and of the laws of cause and
effect. But be that as it may, it is inevitable.

More than fifty years ago, as already stated, there were few
places where the working people of Pudsey could go to, in spending their leisure time, except a place of worship, or the alehouse.
The former was seldom open, while the latter was seldom closed.
And considering the people's taste at that time, the latter had

considerable attraction, in addition to the stimulating effects of the drinks sold there. Churches and chapels at that day were not very attractive. By the Church we mean the State Church, whose adherents did not act in a way towards Dissenters calculated to win their sympathy; for though they had so many favours and advantages, in the shape of national wealth, and royal patronage and privileges, they upheld one of the most unjust and atrocious laws, and made every possible use of it, by which they compelled all those who had either chapels of their own to support, or those who attended neither church nor chapel, to help to pay for the washing of the clergyman's surplice, the ringing of bells, for Church repairs, and for the wine Church people drank at sacrament. Of course we refer to the Church Rate business. Then this Church had wardens (not always moral characters) who during service strolled about the village and footpaths taking by force such as they deemed great sinners to the Church. Frequently people's feet were put in the stocks a few hours, for Sabbath breaking, in the presence of hundreds of spectators, passing jocose and often brutal remarks, jeers, and jibes— very much like (but on a smaller scale) the scenes presented at our once public executions.

Then in addition to all this, there was a man called the "Dog-whipper," armed with a long rod, who kept an eye during service on all those boys and young men sinners who might misbehave, and whose business it was to awe or coerce such into apparent reverence, and often would he walk to and fro in the church, to correct delinquents, by letting his long rod fall on the head of some unfortunate sinner with audible effect. But if the transgressor should be on his guard, and manage to bob his head at the proper time, the rod came in forcible contact with the pew, making a noise that echoed through the empty spaces of the vast edifice, causing a general titter or suppressed laugh. To us at that time the whole State Church machinery seemed a harsh, cruel, vindictive, and slavish affair, without a redeeming feature to win the reverence and affection of one not unmanned by cowardice; and we could not help thinking, that were it not the State Church—patronised by the rich and mighty—as well as the cheapest one afloat, very few would have paid much attention to it.

A comrade of ours, whose parents insisted upon his going to Pudsey church, pressed us to go with him there. He was a good-hearted young man, having nothing really bad about him, though he both amused and annoyed us during most of the service by talking to make us laugh. Amongst other things, he wished that church was his, he would fill it with looms and jennies, reserving

spaces for bartrees, bobbin wheels, baskets of slubbing, etc.,
pointing out where he would place them all. We could not help
laughing at the idea, though annoyed as well, for we never felt
it right to misbehave in either chapel or church.

There are some still living in Pudsey who can never forget the
bad feeling and animosity bred and perpetually kept up by the
annual imposition of the Church Rate. Men who but for that
might have lived together as friends and neighbours ought, were
made enemies, and all done in the name of religion too. Such
barefaced robbery made a deep impression on our own mind at
the time, and we never could feel comfortable in this domineer-
ing Church. It always appeared a kind of Inquisition, or prison
house, for where people are compelled to go as a place of punishment, such can never have much attraction for a thoughtful-
minded person; and as we remarked not long since in an article
on "Political Immorality" we now reassert, by giving the following brief extract:—

"From my boyhood's days such unjust conduct produced a
strong aversion to the State Church in my mind, and no doubt
it has been the same with tens of thousands. I never could feel
comfortable in the Church of England from my knowledge of
its doings. Whereas when in America I visited every church in
the city of Wilmington, both those belonging to the free negroes,
and those of the white people, of every sect and creed, from the
Catholic to the heretical Hicksite Quaker, feeling at home in all
of them, including the Episcopalian Church. Because I knew the
last named Church was content to be on a level with others; its
adherents being willing to pay for their own worship, and to
mix as equals with those outside their own sect, as we seldom
see them do here, where men are puffed up with pride, arrogance,
and self-conceit—arising from the knowledge that their Church
is the one patronised by Parliament, King, Queen, and aristocracy, and that Dissenters are a kind of heretics."

The impression made on our mind when young was, that the
people who went to Pudsey church were *not religious folks at all*
if religion meant equity, and they said they were poor miserable
sinners and did what they ought not, and we believed them.
They appeared to us usurpers of power, hard and cruel dictators,
gathering where they had not sown. To this day we have strong
feelings of dissent from the Church, and he would have to be an
exceptional clergyman we could think it right to spend time in
hearing—one whom we knew to be willing to do unto others as
he would like to be done by in reference to the Establishment
and Disestablishment. Such there are, and to such we have
listened with pleasure.

It was therefore the "Chapel folks," as they were called, we
noticed most, to learn something about religion; for notwithstand-

ing our youthfulness we knew that they had to pay for their own religion—except any voluntary subscriptions outsiders might give.

What then was the impression made on our mind at the time? We answer it was this: Though we did not see much to make us *dread* them as we might a constable, or the State Church, we saw very little to *attract*. Many who went to chapel did not seem to like it, and were pleased when service was over. They did not appear to be as happy as those who stayed away. Our impression was that those who attended chapels did so because they dared not stay away, for fear of future consequences. They talked about this being a "poor, miserable world," a "waste howling wilderness," a "vale of tears," and looked as if religion had more thorns and briars than roses in its path, and that their way was harder than that of the transgressor. Religion was with most of them as if a constant penance. God was seldom spoken of as a Father, let alone as both "father and mother too," as the great Theodore Parker would say. He was represented as austere, stern, jealous, despotic, cruel, and revengeful. Religion was seldom said to be better for this life, apart from any promise of future rewards after death. It seemed to have no object of present utility, and there was no idea of making earth a Paradise; only of escaping some very hot place after death, and receiving a golden crown. Young men full of life and energy might well dread it, and stand aloof, remaining sinners, and run the risk of escaping ultimate consequences by death-bed repentance, which they were told was possible at the eleventh hour—all that was required was faith, not works, they being "filthy rags." There was therefore very little stress laid on virtue and morality and much laid on having correct opinions. Nearly all the prayers at prayer-meetings were centred on self—to be saved from the wrath to come—from the bottomless pit—prepared for the devil and his angels. To young men of courage religion appeared a cowardly affair—a mere dread of eternal burnings after death. Learning was despised; the philosophers

"Bacon, Locke, and Boyle,"

were called

"Wasters of the midnight oil."

Young men were discouraged in learning to speak and write their own language, and told it was pride and worldly wisdom. Science was discouraged, being spoken of as wanting to be "wise above what was written." Men boasted of being readers of only "One Book"—the Bible—except Wesley's or Watts' hymns, which were frequently quoted as texts of Scripture without the persons who did it being aware of the fact. If a young man who had joined one of the religious societies was anxious to understand the fundamental doctrines, and happened to meet with doubts and difficulties, he was told his doubts were from the devil and his carnal reason, and he must "pray them away"—ask God to give him faith to believe what appeared unreasonable. A hundred other matters of this sort might be mentioned, all tending to make religion uninviting, dark, and cold—a kind of calamity; but as some thought, to be endured for the sake of future rewards, not present.

Well, but what do we mean by all this? We mean that though the same creeds and Bible, or most of them, are still there, today a modified meaning is attached—a different interpretation given to the same phraseology, creeds, and texts. Both Methodists, Baptists, and Independents, as well as other sects called Evangelical and Orthodox, teach a very different theology to what they taught fifty years ago, and we rejoice that it is so. Even the State Church, whose creed is controlled by Parliament, but we are aware is no criterion to go by, has clergymen all sworn to teach the same creeds, etc., and yet contains in it men who teach an almost infinite variety of doctrine and dogma, and scarcely two clergymen agree with each other. We have High Church, Low Church, and Broad Church, with endless different degrees in each—like its master the Parliament, it contains all sorts of creeds, from Agnostics to Papists. The other orthodox sects (so called) tells us through their various published organs that they have given too much attention to teaching and preaching Christ's divinity, and too little to His humanity, which is a nearer approach to Unitarianism. They have modified their views about the Atonement, a material hell, and a personal devil, and numerous other doctrines. Many men are allowed to be members of the various sects in Pudsey who would have been summarily expelled for their heresy over thirty years ago. Grammar, once sneered at, is encouraged; science, once called worldly wisdom, is more encouraged; professors of religion are taking a more active part in politics, and in other social movements—are taking a greater interest in, and giving greater attention to measures having for their object the happiness of the people in this life. It is becoming more so everywhere, and Pudsey has not been left behind in the march of theology. They have not lost faith in the future, but get something more substantial as they pass along. Professors of religion today are more of the mind of Betsey in Will Carleton's "Betsey and I are out." Betsey's husband says:—

"We arg'ed the thing at breakfast, we arg'ed the thing at tea,
And the more we arg'ed the question, the more we didn't agree;
And so that heaven we arg'ed no nearer to us got,
But it gave us a taste of something a thousand times as hot."

But Betsey and her husband made all right again, and he tells
us how they "made it up" in the matter of religion as follows:—
"And she said in regards to heaven, we'd try to learn its worth,
By starting a branch establishment, and running it here on
earth."

Chapels now are more inviting—have better music—service of
song, which cannot help being attractive to the young as well
as beneficial to all. They have sewing classes, bazaars, concerts,
and the drama; cricket and football clubs, and harriers; societies
for mutual improvement, and excursions to the seaside. Whereas
at the time we refer to the idea of a religious society having a
cricket or football club would have been looked upon as from
the devil; and the idea of "Wesleyan Harriers" would have been
voted down without a dissentient, as being very awful and wicked
indeed. The case of a man we knew well in our boyhood's days
was a fair sample of all the most conscientious Methodists of that
day. He thought it wrong to whistle even a hymn on Sunday,
wrong for children to romp, jump, shout or laugh heartily on
that day—which reminds us of a law amongst the Puritans of
New England prohibiting a man from kissing his wife from Saturday to Monday. These most conscientious men we knew acted as
if religion was a penance, and as if God would be pleased by
people making themselves miserable. They walked more slowly on
Sundays than on weekdays, and hardly looked aside for anything. They dared not take a walk in Nature's healthy fields to
watch the primrose grow, listen to the towering lark, or to get
a little fragrant hawthorn blossom. How changed is all this!
And what a proof it is of progress in what tends to enoble life
and make it a blessing worth living.

Again, there is not that intolerance amongst different religious
sects towards each other as there was once in Pudsey. Less denouncing of each other's creeds and opinions, a more liberal
spirit pervading all; there is more charity than there once was.

Ministers of religion have more liberty both from congregations
and from Conferences. Forty years ago, a Methodist minister
dared not speak at temperance meetings (at least it was said
so); but if they dared, yet so few did that it was worse still. Both
Mechanics' Institutes and Temperance Societies were spoken of
as tending to infidelity, and as leading people to trust in their
own efforts, and to being puffed up with self-righteousness and
self-conceit. Many in Pudsey today are looked upon as religious
men and women who even thirty years ago would have been
called infidels.

There is less intolerance and narrowness of spirit amongst
the various religious denominations towards those who stand

aloof from all the churches and chapels, heretical scientists, and other great writers. To show what we mean we will give a few brief extracts from an address delivered on the 20th of November, 1885, by the Rev. J. Welford to the students at the Primitive Methodist College, in Manchester, which may be found reported in the *Primitive Methodist World* of the 26th of that month. The report states that the Quarterly Meeting of the Manchester Theological Institute Committee was held on Friday the 20th of November, and at the close of the official business a most interesting address was delivered by the Rev. J. Welford to the students; subject, "Students' life in relation to modern religious thought." It was highly appreciated by all present, and the warmest thanks of the meeting were tendered to Mr. Welford, who was requested to publish the address in one of the Connexional papers, to which request he assented. Mr. Welford recognised the gravity of the occasion, and the importance of weighing well his words. The times were critical for all students, but especially for students of theology. Their position was difficult, and he did not envy the man who had the responsibility of guiding their studies. He needed to combine the spirit of reverence with the spirit of freedom. They must recognise the change that had come over religious thought. Sermons that would do for the town would not always be suitable for the country. They must always be making new sermons. Modern controversies centred round the person and history of Jesus Christ. Old controversies about God and extent of the Atonement, and so on, were dead, and they need not try to revive them. Butler's Analogy was out of date. Paley's Evidences they might put on the top shelves of their libraries. His arguments were destitute of vital force, as a corpse, and only showed on how little a man might win a great reputation. They had to deal with a very different class of men from the old Deists. The great lights of today they had to do battle against were such as Spencer, Tyndall, Arnold, Huxley, Renan, and Harrison. Men who were not Atheists—not coarse Infidels or immoral scorners of the truth; but men of pure life and irreproachable character, and sincere according to their light. Some of these were "Agnostics" who did not deny God, but said they knew nothing about Him. Some of them were "Positivists," and declared the seen and sensible to be the limit of our knowledge, etc. They could not fight the battle of today with the weapons of the eighteenth century. He did not recommend them directly to attack the modern phases of unbelief in the pulpit; the less of it the better. Their reading and experience were not so wide as some of them, and they might be startled to find that some of the truths they had taken for granted had very little foundation on which to rest, and a great part of their theologies had better never have been written, as they had been fruitful in making sceptics. He wanted a theology—they needed one; but it must be of the New Testament and of Jesus Christ, and not of the theologians. There needed a reunion of theology and common sense. In their theologies they had got too far away from Christ and common sense. Jesus lived as He taught. Their theologians sat in armchairs, comfortable colleges and studies, surrounded by libraries of books, and sunk so low that no mortal could follow them, or soared high into regions their visions could not reach. Men now asked for bread and the theologians gave them a stone, or a hard nut which their common grinders were unable to crack. Theologians had made infidels, etc., etc.

We never expected living to hear or read such a liberal and rational address by any orthodox minister, and less still as coming from a Primitive Methodist minister, and being applauded too by all who heard it, and a request made that it should be published in one of the Connexional papers. A generation since the Primitive Methodists were looked upon and spoken of as below all the other sects in culture. This Mr. Welford proves himself an honest and faithful as well as a liberal-minded man, who takes in the whole situation; and has done a noble and worthy work in speaking out well-known facts in regard to "Modern Religious Thought." For we fear that many ministers of religion, who see as Mr. Welford does, keep their thoughts to themselves and their class, and never publish them to the world. After all, these various schools of religious, or rather heterodox, thinkers have modified much of the old theology, and a very different kind is taught in the various pulpits of Pudsey, as elsewhere. What Mr. Welford told the students of Manchester is sunshine in a clear sky, compared with the old narrow, intolerant, and dogmatic theology taught when we were young. We are glad to find that Primitive Methodists instead of being behind other religious denominations called Evangelic, are not so, but are wide awake as to what is going on in the world. If young men had seen and heard what we have, like ourselves they would wonder at hearing a Methodist minister say that Agnostics and Positivists were sincere, lovers of the truth as they saw truth, and that they were moral and high-minded men. When the various religious sects all possess this large-mindedness and feeling of fairness towards those outside all churches, who stand aloof from honest conviction, the days of "boycotting" and persecution for opinions' sake will be at an end, and no heretics (so called) will have a right to complain of religion on that account, and cannot have such a strong feeling of antagonism against what they may not agree with in the various sects and creeds. In concluding this article we propose to notice some of the agencies and influences which in Pudsey have specially tended to break down some of the old dogmatism and effected theological progress. Young men who have to a large extent been born into this new state of things, cannot be aware of what had been going on to effect such a change.

From forty to fifty years ago, Robert Owen, the great Socialist, and one of the most benevolent men that ever lived—however much we may differ from his theories and principles—was propagating his system, with many able advocates assisting him. One of them was the well-known Lloyd Jones, who died a short time since at the age of seventy-five, having done so much for Co-operation and Trades' Unions—and they made some stir in the country. These Socialists in matters of theology were called great infidels, as they charged Christianity with being the cause of many of the evils in society. There were some Owenites in Pudsey, and others who attended their meetings to hear the new system explained, and much discussion took place between the Socialists and the Christians in the village.

The great Joseph Barker, minister in the Methodist New Connexion, came out as an opponent of Owenism, and as a defender of New Testament Christianity. He lectured against it in various parts of the country, wrote pamphlets on the "Abominations of Socialism," held public discussions with its advocates, besides attending to his ministerial duties. Mr. Barker would not engage to defend creeds, but defended only Christianity as taught in the New Testament, and said nothing about the fundamental principles or doctrinal parts; he presented the precepts of Jesus and the Apostles, showing how they would make this earth a Paradise if reduced to practice. The position he felt himself compelled to take in opposing the Socialists no doubt tended to make him heterodox, and he was expelled from the Methodist New Connexion for not being sound in the faith. We wish we could give a more lengthy account of the various movements which have helped to effect theological progress in Pudsey. If, however we did not give a brief sketch of Joseph Barker, any remarks we might make under the above heading would be very deficient. We have seen what pretends to be a Life of this man, written we believe by a nephew of Mr. Barker, but it falls far short of showing the man as he really was. Joseph Barker was a native of Bramley, which joins Pudsey, and in many respects was the same as if he had been a native of the latter place. He was born of poor parents, and often suffered hunger when a boy—for which he always blamed the "wicked Corn Laws," which made trade bad and bread scarce and dear. He managed to get a little learning, though he was largely dependent on his own self-help. At first he joined the old Methodists, and then that branch from which he was expelled as above stated. He had a broad chest, was well built, about the middle height; a large and well-developed head, dark hair, bilious temperament, was calm under great provocation; had a thorough command of the Saxon language, and was able to make himself understood by the most illiterate; which, combined with his calmness and self-control, made him one of the most popular men ever known—both as a writer, preacher, and public debater.

More than forty-five years ago, we heard Mr. Barker for the first time preach in Bradford, when on his way from the North to the Halifax Conference, which expelled him. The large chapel was crowded in every part; he had a minister to give out the hymns, while he sat behind in the pulpit writing a reply to one of the leading men in the Connexion, which he wished to be printed the same night ready to be distributed to the Conference the following day. We had read some of his writings and had been delighted with them, but had never seen him or heard him preach. Such a preacher he proved to be as we had never heard! So calm and self-possessed! no affectation, but spoke as a man speaking to men. No assumed airs, no *mouthing;* no difference in appearance or countenance in the pulpit than when out of it, and dressed as plainly as a Quaker. His sermons all dealt with practical matters of everyday life. He maintained that the religion of Jesus as taught in the New Testament if reduced to practice would make earth a heaven—which was not a common doctrine at that day, as we have before shown. "The common people heard him gladly," and many on leaving the chapel after service might be heard saying, "Never man spake like this man."

When expelled he wrote, travelled, preached, lectured, and debated almost day and night; for he had a constitution of iron, was a great teetotaller, a great enemy to smoking, to which previously he had been a perfect slave. He issued tracts and pamphlets on his principles, defending himself against the Conference, etc., and so rapidly that it was almost a miracle how he could get time to write them. He abandoned all human creeds, adopting the Bible as his only rule of faith and practice; then gave up the common notion of the Atonement, the Deity of Christ, salvation by faith alone and total birth or natural depravity, eternal torments, personality of the devil, a hired ministry and public prayer, but spoke strongly against war and intemperance, as well as other popular wrongs and vices.

There had been a great revival of religion in the New Connexion society at Pudsey before Barker's expulsion, and a large number of promising young men had become members. The lectures of Finney, the great American Revivalist, had been much read by the advice of William Trotter, a preacher in the Connexion, who preached occasionally at Pudsey, being stationed in the same Circuit as it was in. He was a most earnest and powerful young man, exposing vices of all kinds, striking important truths right home to his hearers. After describing sins and sinners minutely, he would point his finger, looking intently at his hearers, saying, *"I mean thee, sinner; our message is to thee, and not someone else not here."* His manner was quite dramatic, his looks and gestures all tended to rivet the attention of all who heard him, and large numbers were added to the society. After his preaching he had a prayer meeting, and all anxious inquirers were requested to stay at the meeting and come to a penitent form. If anyone should pray to God for faith, Trotter would shout: "He will never give you faith; God has give His word and promise, cannot you believe Him?" Now this man Trotter was expelled by Conference along with Barker, and they worked together. They were joined by one Thomas Smith, whose great theme was the "Wealth Question," and who believed it wrong to lay up treasure on earth. Such works as Harris's prize essay "Mammon," were much read. Barker, however, was soon found to be too heretical for Trotter and Smith, who left him and joined the "Plymouth Brethren," and were very little heard of after.

When Conference expelled Mr. Barker there was a split throughout the Methodist New Connexion. Most of the Pudsey members left the Conference party, and there began such a commotion, revolution, and agitation, mixed with such bitterness of spirit, as no one not mixed up with it can imagine. Those who thought Barker was in the right were called "Barkerites," though they never accepted the term, but simply called themselves "Christians"; though for convenience we may use the term for the present. Many belonging to other religious societies in Pudsey became Barkerites; many also were expelled by the old Methodists and Primitives; while others left to avoid expulsion for their Barkerite heresies.

For some time the Barkerites had the chapel in Pudsey, but there was no peace between what was called the "old and the new schools of thought"; and after a time some having gone back to what was called the "flesh pots of Egypt" the Reformers left, and met at houses or in rooms, reading and investigating the Scriptures, speaking as each one thought. Most of them had

Reference Bibles, and some had Greek Lexicons. They tested the prevailing orthodox doctrines by Scripture, and found them—as they thought—without the least authority. A number of those young men had been class-leaders, local preachers, and exhorters before the split, and for several summers, mostly on the Sunday mornings, they started with their Reference Bibles and a little lunch in their pockets, walking twenty or thirty miles sometimes, speaking at several villages during the day, challenging and answering questions; or, on meeting opposition, were often seen after dark eight or ten miles from home, standing up debating with the orthodox people, quoting or reading from the New Testament by the light of a candle. They were all teetotallers, and ate their bit of lunch on the road, drinking water from the spring, except sometimes a kind friend pressed them to take tea. They generally contrived to be near some chapel or church when service concluded, and read out aloud some startling passages from the prophets, such as "The kind of fasts the Lord required," etc., or denounced the orthodox doctrines, so as to induce a hearing from the people, and to have discussions, which they felt to be their *forte*. These "Evangelical Reformers," as they called themselves, held meetings at Bramley, Armley, Wortley, Farnley, Leeds, Holbeck, Hunslet, Castleford, Pontefract, Beeston, Churwell, Gildersome, Tong, Cockersdale, Drighlington, Adwalton, Birstall, Birkenshaw, Gomersal, Cleckheaton, Heckmondwike, Batley, Dewsbury, Halifax, Sowerby Bridge, Amblethorne, Northowram, Shelf, Wyke, Lowmoor, Wibsey, Bowling, Thornton, Bradford, Shipley, Bingley, Baildon, Calverley, Stanningley, Farsley, Rodley, Horsforth, Otley, etc., and often returned home almost exhausted, for there were no railroads they could make use of, and if there had been, they were too poor to pay for riding. Whatever may be thought as to their wisdom, they were earnest and sincere in what they did, and they thoroughly found one thing, viz., that ministers of the Gospel, as well as other professors of religion who opposed them, were intensely ignorant of the Bible, often quoting orthodox phrases, parts of creeds, old sayings, and even Wesley's hymns, as texts of Scripture, proving that they either did not read the Bible or only did so as a duty, with no idea of searching and understanding its contents. On the other hand, the Reformers had so read, conversed, and compared various texts and teachings of the Bible as to know at once where any passage was to be found, as well as its context. There were large numbers of these young apostles who went about the country, speaking in the open-air in favourable weather, and agreeing to meet each other at places; some of these were able to hold their own in debate against allcomers.

The late R. M. Carter, M.P., who was in poor circumstances at the time, was one, and took a prominent part in advocating Evangelical Reform.

The Barkerites in Pudsey, as in other places, had much to suffer for their principles; many lost their work, and others were refused as workmen, because it was said they were infidels, and "denied the Lord that bought them."

In course of time, after meeting together in houses and hired rooms, the Reformers invited the Unitarians to send them preachers and lecturers, which they did, till at length they built the present Unitarian chapel.

Now, it was not the number of converts made by the Owenites, Barkerites, or Unitarians, but the influence each and all had on the various religious bodies, the thousands of pamphlets scattered about, lent, given, and sold, and the everyday discussions carried on in the village, that made people's minds more liberal and rational without their being aware of it, and we repeat that today there are scores of persons, members of orthodox sects, whose views are such that even thirty years ago they would have been expelled for "not being sound in the faith."

Barker's most difficult work was in getting people to think for themselves. But many did so, and therefore did not keep changing —at least, not backwards and forwards as he did. They learnt not only to prove orthodox writers, but Barker himself, as he had taught them. He was the means of influencing professors of religion to take a greater part in social and political matters tending to mend this world, by raising men on earth by temperance and virtue.

In addition to the above-named influences there has also been the general and widespread one exerted by such men as Darwin, Spencer, Huxley, Tyndall, Renan, Colenso, Harrison, Arnold, Mill, Dr. Channing, and Theodore Parker, for their works have been read in Pudsey, and extracts and reviews of most of them have appeared in the newspapers and other journals, and the result is that Pudsey, along with Mr. Welford quoted above, has been rationalised and benefited. Besides, there has been the general march of intelligence on every subject, and it is impossible for theology to escape the influence. In the future it will be more so, and Pudsey will take its share in the progress which is going on, and will continue to go on for ever, in spite of all the creeds and conferences in Christendom.

This Joseph Barker did not stop at evangelical reform. After taking the Bible as a rule of faith and practice, he said it was not infallible, but was a "false guide in some things, and a double-tongued director," and fell back on reason and common sense, still using what he thought the best parts of the Bible. The Unitarians gave him a printing press, and he came to Wortley, and issued waggon loads of heretical pamphlets; he also published a political paper called *The People,* in which he went far ahead of the "People's Charter." He recommended emigration to America, went there, bought land, farmed, and lectured as well as held a long discussion in Philadelphia with the famous Doctor Bergg. After some time he returned to England an "Agnostic," having no faith in God or a future life, had a discussion with Thomas Cooper, in Bradford, on "The Being of a God," was joint editor of the *National Reformer* along with Charles Bradlaugh, had a difference with him, wished to be sole editor, but the shareholders elected Bradlaugh. Then Barker began a paper of his own *The Review,* and began to advocate a liberal religion again, took sides with the Southern slaveholders, when the war between the North and South began, changed his politics, said there was no such thing as men's or women's rights and that *"might was the only right."* He wished to join the Unitarians, but was not encouraged in that quarter; so he joined the Primitive Methodists, for whom he preached and lectured in various parts of the country, but he had not his former fervour and eloquence, and his once black hair had turned white. Thus, this most wonderful man, with such rare abilities, described a circle from East to South, West, North, and back again to the East, making as many stopping places between each cardinal point. His great fault was that when he differed from persons in opinion he defamed their characters, instead of distinguishing between men and principles. He called the Socialists "filthy brutes," and both teachers and practisers of the "vilest abominations," and after he was expelled by the Conference, he wrote many pamphlets to prove that the leading men, both lay and clerical, in the New Connexion, were the vilest characters on earth. He at first extolled the Unitarians, then wrote a pamphlet to cover them with shame and obloquy. It was the same with regard to the anti-slavery men in America—the Philadelphia and English Secularists, first praising them as being unequalled for their intelligence and virtue, then holding them up as being ignorant and despicable. He went to America, and died there, making a statement in writing on his death bed, about his faith in the Christian religion, which was nothing more than most Unitarians might have made. Joseph Barker was never sound in the faith, tested by human creeds, even when a minister of the New Connexion; nor when he died, for when using *orthodox* phraseology he attached a *heterodox* meaning to it. But in spite of all his errors and faults, he did much good, by way of stirring people's minds, making them exercise their own judgment, and teaching them self-dependence.

In our next letter we purpose saying something more on the woollen business in Pudsey, and other changes of employment as well.

CHAPTER XIII

Contributory Causes of Change and Progress in the Manufacture of Woollens

Our purpose—What it is, and what it is not—Recapitulation of processes—Australian wool—Its history—Mungo—Cotton warps—Predictions falsified—Piece dyeing—Burl dyeing—Fancy Coatings—Great increase in the number of woollen manufacturers—"Hawking Cloth," and Cloth Hawkers—Many clothmakers begin to finish their goods—Leeds Cloth Hall is deserted, and Company Mills decay.

In our Chapters VI, VII, and VIII, we have already dealt briefly with the manufacture of woollen cloths in Pudsey—promising to return to the subject later on.

Our object was stated not to deal with this branch exhaustively, or in all its bearings, but only with some of its leading features, to give the young folks a general idea of what their forefathers were doing at the time referred to, so that by comparing the past with the present they might see the change, and, as we thought, progress, which had been made.

At one time the one-spindled bobbin wheel was seen to have been a most important machine, till it was superseded by the spinning jenny, which began to wind the weft it spun on to the bobbin, and the jenny itself after being enlarged in its number of spindles was displaced by the mule. We endeavoured to represent old-time clothmaking and clothmakers as we remembered seeing them, with their notions, habits, and customs of that day. Moiting wool by hand, "lecking" pieces, "wetting bobbins" with the old wooden tube called a "bobbin sahker," were also noticed. The rapid increase of manufacturers, and the making of a greater variety of goods, were referred to; and the custom of hand-loom weavers doing so much work for nothing, called "old jobbing," came in for some share of consideration. We also noticed the once great institution of "burling cloth," and peeped into an old-time burling house, and heard what was going on there. The slubbers we saw were once a most important class of men in the eyes of the public, and in their own especially, but the slubber in time was displaced altogether by the condenser, and he who went up like a rocket came down like a stick, when that great and sudden change took place, never to be forgotten by any one who survived the shock. We mentioned the introduction of Cape and Australian wools, and propose now to refer to a few of the principal factors which contributed in effecting the change and progress in the woollen branch in Pudsey.

The easier it is to produce an article by increased facilities, and more likely is the business producing it to be developed. The rapid increase in the growth of Australian wools helped to stimulate the manufacture of woollen goods.

It is not eighty years since the first wool was brought to this country from New South Wales. In the year 1808, a Mr. Marsden brought ten or twelve stones to London, and offered it to the well-known Thompsons, of Rawdon, on condition that they would make it into cloth: they were to have it for nothing, except paying the carriage from London. This firm did so at their mill, which is not far from where we write this, and it proved much better than they expected; George the Third had a coat made off the piece of cloth manufactured. At that time such wool was worthless in the colony, and was used for bedding, and seen scattered about anywhere and wasted. It was a long time before any of this wool was used for woollens, there being a strong prejudice against it. Mr. Wood, of Bradford, began to use a little by mixing it with other wools for worsted goods; but about sixty years ago there was only imported 1,500,000 pounds, and none of it was used for woollen goods. But now only think of the quantity sold annually in London alone, in addition to what is imported by other countries direct from the colonies; probably as many bales as there were pounds sixty years ago. Of course the breed of sheep has been much improved, as that also of Cape wools has, the latter for some time was full of burrs and kemps. What would have become of the manufacture of woollen goods either in Pudsey or elsewhere had there been no colonial wools?

Another great factor in the progress of woollen manufacturing was

MUNGO

which means woollen rags after they have been torn to pieces by a machine, and reduced to the original wool fibre. It is said by some that it got its name from the man who first introduced it, who said "It mun go," meaning "It must go!"

The prejudice at first against it was somewhat legitimate, because from the ignorance of not knowing how to mix it with proper wools, or to scribble it properly when mixed, a very tender thread was produced, and much poor work for both spinners and weavers was the result, as well as unsound cloth made. But now the art of using this article, as well as all kinds of short waste, has attained something like perfection, for there are machines by which almost every bit of fibre can be utilised, and the strength of thread and cloth maintained.

Another impulse, or rather impetus, was given to the woollen branch by

COTTON WARPS

for mungo then could be more easily used, when only in the weft. Many might be heard saying that both mungo and cotton warps would have their day, that cotton had no elasticity in it, and would break, and that if persisted in, England would lose all her trade, as foreigners would never buy a second time after proving our goods. A large number of manufacturers refused for a long time to use anything but pure, unadulterated new wools. What a change has taken place! What a large quantity of mungo, shoddy, and waste of every description is now made up, and cotton warps as well, in England, and made into sound, service-able, and cheap clothing, too—stronger than many goods were formerly when made of all wool. This is owing to the superior machinery now in use, and the advanced knowledge there is now in mixing, etc. At one time there was such a large demand for low cotton warp meltons that even butchers and grocers began to make them. It required very little skill, a little wool and mungo or waste to get certain shades of mixture sent to the Company mills and returned in weft on bobbins, a few cotton warps, hand-loom weavers to weave them, and sample pieces would be shown and sold in a week or two after.

But the mania was only temporary, though cotton warps are still made in large quantities, and both they and mungo are as likely to go as ever. At the present time a large quantity of cotton is used by mixing it with wool, so that it is not easy to detect. All these various discoveries and uses have tended to promote the manufacture of woollens.

We remember the time when dyeing woollen cloths in the piece was introduced, but this process was very badly managed at first, the goods being made tender in the boiling and especially in burl-dyeing. Ultimately, however, the difficulties were overcome, and making cloths in grey or white, to dye in the cloths various shades (both cotton warps and all-wools), became a great busi-ness, so that a large amount of the labour of women kept by cloth finishers was dispensed with. Their business was to burl cloths partly finished by covering the burls with ink. But what with piece and burl-dyeing, extracting the vegetable matter, and the introduction of the moiting machine, together with a con-siderable decline in the demand for highly faced goods, the old-time burlers and burling houses referred to before, which formerly were to be seen almost everywhere in Pudsey, are now comparatively unknown.

What are called fancy coatings began to be made on a large scale about twenty years ago. After a while quite a new class of goods to some extent were made, called "worsted coatings," though the latter we believe have not been largely made in Pudsey; but it is a great business, and those who went into it at first did well.

Those who had made plain goods predicted that both fancy cloths and worsted coatings would soon "end their days," and that plain faced goods would be as much wanted as ever. But that time appears to be far off, for there is no end to the variety of designs possible in fancy woollens and worsteds.

Perhaps Pudsey had never so many small manufacturers of woollens as it had from twenty to thirty years ago, and Leeds had never so many large and small merchants. The once famous Coloured Cloth Hall began to cease, being an index as to the amount of business done in Leeds. Large numbers of small and needy manufacturers, both from Pudsey and other manufacturing villages, might be seen both on market days—but mostly off those days—carrying sample pieces from place to place trying to effect sales. In addition to these there was quite an army of men called "cloth hawkers," who spent every day in the week showing makers' goods. These men got one shilling for each end of cloth from the merchant who bought, and the same from the maker. Some of them did well, making much money, and others might, had they been sober, steady characters, which was not always the case. The making of fancy goods also tended to bring the Leeds Cloth Hall into disrepute, because makers would not like to expose to each other their various designs. Then some makers began to finish their own goods, and did not make use of the Hall. These changes, together with others which tended to centralise the woollen business in fewer hands, making it impossible for small makers to compete with large ones who had large capital and machinery of their own, not only rendered useless the Leeds Cloth Hall (which has since been used for Wombwell's Wild Beast Show) but also struck a heavy blow at

COMPANY MILLS

which had been erected in Pudsey in every part of the town. As Company Mills on the old principle, they have seen their day, and as such are at a discount. Some have become the property of large manufacturers, while others have been used for other manufactures than woollens. Some no doubt there will be who will be ready to say that what we have stated above proves decay rather than progress. We, however, think differently, since there

is every proof, notwithstanding the hard up-hill work of many
of its inhabitants, that as a whole they are far better off now
than they were either sixty, fifty, forty, thirty, or twenty years
ago, though the present is an exceptionally depressed time, and
yet not to be mentioned as such, compared with the bad times
fifty or even forty years ago. We will go further, and assert that
had the manufacture of woollen cloths left Pudsey altogether,
that of itself would not prove it had not made progress. The condition of its inhabitants now and formerly is the proper test. In
our next chapter we shall deal with the revolution caused by the
introduction of power-looms, and the partial change of the business in Pudsey.

CHAPTER XIV

Power Looms, and the Revolution they Effected

No progress without decay—Machinery and its effects—Strong opposition to power-looms—Blackburn, Bradford, and Leeds—A curious petition to Parliament—The old hand-loom weaver's lament—"To be sold by Auction"—Great depreciation of value in property—"The darkest cloud has a silver lining"—Manufacturers have to buy their own machinery and pay for all odd jobbing—The Worsted Business—The Boot and Shoe Trade and the revolution in that branch—"Cobblers" and old-time boot and shoemakers.

Without decay there can be no progress in manufacturing; hence every new process displaces the old, and every new machine in advance renders useless the ruder sort. It is quite natural for those men whose labour is superseded to look upon improvement as decay itself, and to some extent it is so in relation to themselves for a time. They forget that though a few may suffer for a time the millions are benefited by cheaper goods produced; as well as those who tend the new machines having easier work, and mostly earning better wages.

Probably no new machine ever produced such a revolution in the making of various fabrics as the introduction of power-looms has done. Not only in the woollen branch more recently, but more especially in the cotton and worsted branches previously. We have before mentioned the destruction of a thousand power-looms at Blackburn in one week by the exasperated hand-loom weavers there; and in Bradford also great riots took place, and much destruction of property was the result.

Fifty-five years ago Leeds was noted for its manufacture of camlets and stuff goods, and a public meeting was held, convened by both manufacturers and operatives in that department, to protest against the ruinous power-looms. This meeting sent a petition to Parliament with 1500 signatures attached, stating that power-looms inverted Providence and struck at the very existence of the working classes, and that the condition of the hand-loom weaver and his family was wretched in the extreme through the influence of that most injurious of inventions, etc.

It was some time before power-looms for weaving woollen

cloths were introduced, and then very slowly, though it was plain enough to all thoughtful-minded people that the doom of hand-looms was fixed. Many of the old weavers might be heard saying that "power-looms might do for narrow goods such as cottons and stuffs, but never for broad cloths." Meanwhile, unheeded, power-looms for weaving broad cloths steadily marched on, being intro-duced first by one large manufacturer and then another; and it was well for the hand-loom weavers that the introduction was not more rapid, or the shock and suffering for the time would have been much more severe. Slubbers had been displaced, but they were not such a numerous class as the weavers. Spinners on jennies had been superseded by mule spinners, but many of them could weave, and jennies were taken down and looms put up in their places, while some of the most skilful and enterprising learnt to spin on the mule. But when both billy, jenny, and hand-loom were rendered useless, the old weavers saw nothing in the world worth living for, and began to feel there was nothing for them to do. The hand-loom weavers formed a large class of men, and women, as well as boys and girls in their teens. Many years before, when cloths began to be made broader, the old ten and eleven quarter looms had been taken down and put on the "balks" next to the roof, with a strong faith that before long they would be wanted again when the temporary whim was over. But that time never came, and the old looms lay piled there to rot (as cotton and worsted looms had done), and were ultimately used to light the fire, or for other base uses never thought of by their once owners. But in the case of power-looms it was not a question of width or strength of the hand-looms—good, bad, and indif-ferent were all the same. Power-looms spoke as with a voice of thunder to all who had ears to hear: "Get out of our way; ye have had your day; see the march of your superiors."

The change had a terrible effect on the minds of some old hand-loom weavers. Many an old weaver had become as much attached to his favourite loom as a warrior to his old steed, or the owner of "Poor Dog Tray" to his dog. We have seen an old Pudsey weaver with tears in his eyes while looking at and re-counting the good points of his loom. Yes, it was hung on its prods as a loom ought to be, and swung to and fro as a loom should do, the going part easy to put back, yet came freely to its work, and would get any amount of weft in. When that loom first came from one of the best makers in England—all so smooth, sleek, and trim, thirteen quarters wide—he was envied by all who saw it; the neighbours all came to see it, and admired and coveted it. But now for some time both this loom and another which is not to be despised, being much better than the average—

together with a once famous jenny, bartrees, creel, and bobbin wheel—have all been dumb, and are covered with dust and cobwebs. Where once the humming and whizzing of the jenny roller, wheel, and spindles, and the merry clicks of shuttles and thuds of the going parts, were heard mingling with the workers' songs and chorus, all is now still as death.

At length the old weaver dies, and both his favourite loom and all else besides in that old workshop are brought under the auctioneer's hammer—"To be sold to the highest bidder." The auctioneer expatiates on the well-known qualities and capabilities of this famous loom, telling the company this is a loom that can weave anything from six quarters to twelve, will weft either light or heavy; that while some have to weight their "gallow balks" and put the prods forward for wefting, this never requires altering; that while some weavers had to "lake" because their looms were not broad or good enough to weave the best cloths, the owner of that loom had never missed a web on that account, as everybody knew that loom could weave all kinds; he asks for a bid, but no one ventures. The neighbours look on sympathisingly, and strangers wonderingly; while the unfeeling and calculating brokers laugh outright, telling the auctioneer nobody wants "poverty knocking hand-looms," and that he might as well offer quills and tinder boxes to those who have steel pens and lucifer matches. It proves so; for after having but a few shillings bid, this famous loom is knocked down, and will probably soon be sawn up to bear the roof of some old coal-house or pig-cote, or may be chopped up for firewood. If anything could have moved the old hand-loom weaver's corpse in its grave, the disgraceful end of his famous loom would certainly have done it. Large mill owners talk about the depreciation of their machinery, but which of them ever experienced such a depreciation as was suffered in the above case? Considering the rent for the loom while standing and the cost of selling it, it was worse than if given away when the last web was "felled." Hundreds of men who were poor, but had been in the habit in the worst of times of looking with honest pride on the capital invested in their looms and jenny, have lost all in the end.

We are sometimes told that the darkest cloud has a silver lining, and we have seen the horizon suddenly covered with a dense black cloud, which rose higher and higher till it spread and covered the whole canopy, and ultimately the whole heavens, and made all so dark that we had to light lamps, candles, or gas to see what was going on. But behind that expansive and dense cloud the sun shone as ever in all his brilliancy and splendour, and before long the cloud cleared off, and we had the cheering rays of the sun as if nothing had happened. So it is in this case. There is a bright side as well as a dark one in the matter of power-looms.

In the first place, families are better housed, for when hand-looms were in vogue they occupied the chambers, and the family slept on the stone floors, in parlours or the house; many were often damp and not so healthy. But now the people of the same class occupy the upper rooms with boarded floors, and are more respectable, have more room, and are healthier. Then girls can earn more money on the power-loom the year through, than the average hand-loom weaver could, and with much less exertion too. The minder of the power-loom has only to tie up the threads and healds, and put fresh bobbins into the shuttle. Every part of the loom is adjusted to every other part, as if it were clockwork, and acts with the greatest precision. It appears as if it could hear and feel, so sensitive is it to the slightest flaw; as if it were conscious and knew all that was going on. Besides power-loom weavers have not to buy looms and a jenny to spin for them; or bobbins, flaskets, and baskets; or to pay rent and taxes for them standing; nor candles, or gas and coal for lighting and warming the workshop. They have not to pay for repairs, for all wear and tear, for new wheel bands for the jenny, for steps, laphes (loops), wharles, and for oil to grease with. Nor have they to buy shuttles, pickers, sideboards, shopboards, shuttleboards, picking sticks, and bands and cords; or gears, slays, web sticks, and rattles. They have not to be propped up on the treadles and seatboards, with an artificial handle attached to the going part; or have their wrists bandaged to give strength, as some of them would were they hand-loom weavers. They have not to fetch slubbing, warp their webs, lay up lists, size, put the webs out to dry, seek gears, leck pieces, tenter, teem, dew, and cuttle them; and least of all would they think of breaking wool, scouring, and dyeing it *all for nothing too*. No, it would not do for a power-loom to stand while the weaver did all the "odd jobbing." The employer would be wasting power, so at last the interests of employers and employees are mutual; whereas when a hand-loom stood still it was at the expense of the weaver and not the manufacturer. This new invention has compelled manufacturers to buy all the machinery themselves, and not have weavers and spinners to help them; and also to pay for all odd jobbing they once got done for nothing. There are persons now paid for doing all this work, and no doubt it is better done; and cloths after all are made both cheaper, better, more regular or even and with less trouble and cost. Young people who cannot have the sentiment in this matter that old hand-loom weavers had, will be apt to fall back on reason, and agree with us that considering the many trials and difficulties which beset the hand-loom weavers it was high time the whole system came to an end—even had it been at the cost of the woollen business leaving Pudsey altogether, providing any other business stepped in to take its place, for one could hardly have been introduced as bad as the weaving on hand-looms had become. Many of the most intelligent and aspiring young men had long had our view on hand-loom weaving, and did everything in their power to get away from "poverty knocking," as weaving was called; they succeeded, and improved their condition in life. While with the many improvements in machinery, it requires less skill and laborious management today to run a large mill—converting the raw material into cloths ready for making into garments, than it did once to employ a dozen hand-loom weavers and to have the cloths made properly.

While the manufacture of woollens in Pudsey has progressed in its processes, from the spinning on the wheel one thread at a time to the self-acting mule; and from carding by hand to the broad and many swifted scribblers and condensers; from weaving without pickers and picking stick, or two weaving on a loom, to the power-loom; and now the scouring, moiting, tentering, warping, and milling machines; when everything is done so cheap and economically, and better both for the employer and employed, other kinds of business have been slowly introduced to meet the wants and needs of labour superseded by the new inventions in making woollen cloths.

The worsted business has been introduced and many hands are now employed in that branch. But the most wonderful change produced in Pudsey in any branch of industry is seen in the Boot and Shoe business. Messrs. Scales and Salter, by their untiring industry and close application to business, their great enterprise combined with shrewdness and caution, and free from all ostentation, have done much for the town of Pudsey. And now that the old firm has been made two, there is every prospect, with the young blood there is to carry on both firms, that the already gigantic business will attain much larger proportions in the future. We by no means pretend that Messrs. Scales and Salter did what they did do specially for the benefit of Pudsey, but for themselves in a legitimate and honourable way. Nor did they ever on the other hand display a reckless heedlessness of the welfare of its inhabitants, like many other employers of labour; they aimed at making their business a success, and succeeded. But it so happens that as a rule men cannot raise themselves in business without creating a demand for labour, and thereby conferring a benefit upon others.

We have no need to go back fifty or sixty years to see the great change effected in the boot and shoe business. Perhaps no other industry has been so revolutionised in the same length of time as it; certainly this is true as regards Pudsey. Boots and shoes formerly were only made when bespoke or ordered; the makers kept no stock, except misfits. Many of those called makers did not know how to make, and were cobblers, or menders of shoes. One here and there had a high reputation as a maker, and kept a few hands employed; while others only employed themselves. Of course everything was done by hand, there were no sewing machines. Where a few makers worked together they were generally better posted on the topics of the day than other operatives, because their employment allowed any amount of conversation, and the workshop became a kind of college. But many of these journeymen bootmakers were like the same class of tailors, a very drunken lot, and seldom worked on the Mondays, which caused that day to be called "Cobbler's Monday." Today instead of boots and shoes being made by hand as formerly, scarcely anything is done without a machine, and there is such a division of labour now that there are very few men who could take the leather and without the aid of machinery make a pair of boots; and probably not very many who could perform every part even with machinery, except the principal managers. There are not only more hands employed, but boots and shoes are cheaper, and the whole community gets the benefit.

The sewing machine in Pudsey (as in most other places) has effected much good, both as used by families, and especially by dressmakers and tailors, as well as in the boot and shoe trade. And people who work and tend the machines can both earn and save more than those who formerly did the same work by hand.

The woollen business, like all others, is becoming more centralised, so that it is more difficult for one to begin business with a small capital than formerly, yet the bulk of the people are benefited.

CHAPTER XV
Fulneck

Why we deal with it—A seat of learning—The founders good judges—Its widespread reputation—Pudsey people should feel proud of this settlement—Its efficient day and Sunday schools— Why Fulneck had a charm for us—Its seclusion, music, and people—Contrast between a Methodist revival meeting and the service at Fulneck Chapel—Noisy visitors from Pudsey—Its attractions—A little community.

To talk of Fulneck specially, in its relation to Pudsey, may appear to some out of place, as the former forms part of the latter. But this little colony, Bohemian brotherhood, or Moravian settlement, forms such a distinct community of itself that it deserves separate notice; otherwise our Moravian friends might reasonably object to some of our remarks as not applying to them, though living in Pudsey township.

We remember the time when Fulneck people were not very ready to recognise Pudsey. There was such a disparity betwixt this recognised seat of learning and any of the surrounding villages, as to create a fear lest evil communications should corrupt their good manners; or rather lest their outside patrons should think so, and refuse to send them pupils. However that might be, the first founders proved themselves excellent judges in selecting such a beautiful site on which to erect the various buildings, so well adapted to their wants, and to lay out grounds all so admirably situated. It must at that time have presented no objections to those who had made the selection from the fact of its belonging to Pudsey.

Fulneck has a wide reputation, and is well known for its schools and its efficient educational facilities. It has received pupils from almost every part of the world, and men destined to figure as prominent characters were educated there. The poet and Radical, Montgomery, was one, and many others might be mentioned.

Our remarks as to the low state of education in Pudsey fifty and sixty years ago will not apply to this part of it. How is it likely when giving a high-class education in its schools was the source of its income, and teaching was its profession? The whole atmosphere of Fulneck was that of culture and refinement, and we have no doubt, though so little intercourse took place between the inhabitants of Pudsey generally and those of Fulneck, that the latter have exerted a beneficial influence on the former. We think the Pudsey people should feel grateful and even proud of having such a people as the Moravians in their midst, who have always been harmless, urbane, respectful, and refined, and in every way an honour to the township.

This Moravian settlement did not confine its labours to the colleges or boarding schools, but had day schools at reasonable charges for what would be called middle-class boys, or sons of tradesmen, etc., and some poor people's children, whose parents were Moravians, managed to get a decent education there. Then, fifty-five years ago, Fulneck Sunday school was perhaps unequalled for its efficiency, having excellent discipline and one of the best staff of teachers of any Sunday school in the country.

When very young, Fulneck had a kind of charm for us, and we remember thinking and saying that it always looked like Sunday there, all being so quiet and clean, and most of the people well dressed.

Its situation is all that could be desired, which of itself makes it a lovely place. It is on the south side of Pudsey, about halfway down in the deep valley through which Tong beck winds its course, and commands a pleasant view of the valley and the woodland slopes of Tong, its church, hall, and park; and being well shielded from the cold north winds, its large and beautiful well-kept gardens produce an abundance of flowers, fruits, and vegetables much earlier than could be done on the higher parts of Pudsey. It is a retired and secluded spot, free from the noise and clamour of more densely populated towns and cities, and well adapted to mental pursuits, deep thought, study, and reflection; and we repeat that those who first selected it were not bad judges.

There is much of the communistic principle in operation there. The males and females live mostly apart, except those families who live as labourers and carry on some business in the settlement. The eastern part is for the sisters and the western for the brethren, and the chapel is built in the centre betwixt the two; the females sit on one side of the chapel, and the males on the opposite side.

The Moravians are great lovers of music, and besides the organ have often other instruments as well performing during or in connection with their worship. Their religious services, when we heard them, were refined, solemn, calm, and grand, reminding one of the place the worshippers were aiming at, after having

"shuffled off this mortal coil." We remember once going to Fulneck chapel from the midst of a Methodist revival, about forty-
five years ago, and the calm, soft, steady, sweet, and impressive
character of the service was such as appeared a kind of rebuke to
the earnestness, noise, and uproar of a revival meeting. We remarked at the time that the Fulneck people by their manner
of worshipping seemed to say to the Methodists: "What's all the
row about? Take things easy, brothers: the world is not going to
come to an end all at once; and if it is, all your shouting and turbulence will not prevent it!" We thought also, and said, that the
Moravian style of worshipping appeared as if its adherents were
"paid by the day," and therefore took matters easy, while that
of the Methodists seemed as if they were "paid by the piece," and
hence the zeal, hurry, and bustle displayed by the latter in their
meetings and around the penitent forms. It is but just, however,
to acknowledge that at that time we wondered how the Moravians
could be so calm and unmoved while so many unconverted sinners
were "hanging by the brittle thread of life" over the unquench-
able fire of the bottomless pit, and whose souls, or many of them,
might be "snatched as brands from the burning" by their agency;
though our views since then, we confess, have been considerably
modified.

It was no uncommon thing at the time we refer to for the
quiet and retired Fulneck people to be somewhat disturbed by
the nightly visits of young men from those parts of Pudsey
nearest the settlement. Not that much real mischief was done
or intended, but for a little romping, noise, and clatter, and the
least bawling sounded much louder there on account of the
ordinary extreme quietness of the place. Many no doubt were
attracted to Fulneck at nights by the superb pies, parkins, and
butterscotch made and sold by the confectioner there. This
woman sold penny pies and half-penny parkins, acknowledged
by all to be delicious. Of course our experience when a boy was
necessarily limited in such matters, but we felt certain that it
was impossible for any woman upon earth to make richer or
finer pies and parkins than this woman made and sold, and we
do not remember ever eating any since in all our wanderings
which tasted so good. Though it is possible that whilst we are
young and our experience narrow, and our sense of taste fresh
and not abused, we may form exaggerated notions of such things.
There is another little matter which we may mention, viz., that
Fulneck had a Bakery, as we suppose it has still; for this community had within its settlement, persons of various trades and
callings to supply their needs, without being dependent on the
outside world so much. They had their bakery—a store or shop

where almost everything needed for eating and drinking was kept, and most other articles required in a house; and though the price in some cases was a little higher, some of the people outside the settlement sent there for things, knowing that they were good. There was also a tailor, shoemaker, doctor, &c., and a night watchman. As we were saying, Fulneck had a bakery, and its bread was liked by all. The bread carts passed through Pudsey, or rather through the south and west parts of it, on their way to Bradford. Many children who lived near where the cart passed, attached great importance to it, for they deemed it a famous treat to be able to buy from the cart what was called a "nuketin," costing a halfpenny. It was a triangular cake, or three nooked, hence *"nuketin,"* with a few currants in it—when currants meant something, being at such a high price. Many children we have known to be good and obedient to their parents for a week together to have a halfpenny to buy one of these nuketins, which was both cheap obedience and a sensible and substantial reward.

CHAPTER XVI
Tong

Why we deal with Tong—Surrounding scenery sixty years ago—
Poaching and poachers—The Game Laws—Fetching milk, etc.—
Our early attachments—Rational progress no need to spoil the
scenery—Tong Church bells—Lines, written on hearing them
ring in 1856.

What leads us to make a few remarks on the relationship of
Tong and Pudsey in dealing with progress in the latter place is
the fact that fifty years ago, and less than that, there was strong
temptation on the estate of the former to a few of the inhabitants
of Pudsey. At that time the woods were more dense, and a better
staff of gamekeepers were kept to look after the hares, part-
ridges, and pheasants, than at present (at least this is our impression), but poaching was much more common then.

We knew two classes of poachers; one class would not object
to doing deeds much more mischievous and degrading than
poaching or catching game, while the others were decent men
in other respects, who worked at their calling during the day and
made over hours at night. We have often seen them about sun-
down on the borders of Tong estate, trying to ascertain the
precise locality of game, and later on they went to catch their
prey. Those kept on friendly terms with the farmers, to whom
they occasionally presented part of their spoil. The lower class
of poachers were not very scrupulous, and would take their
trained dogs, air guns, snares and nets; and not content with
catching stray game, would invade the Tong estates as well, and
sometimes take the domestic poultry belonging to farmers and
other private persons from the hen roosts. At that time there
was not all that mining going on through or close to the game
preserves we see now, nor the many tram wagons; and there
were no "rural police" to help large landowners and their keepers
to preserve the game.

Poaching was deemed a crime, and punished as such; though
we very much question whether poachers ever felt any qualms
of conscience for having caught a hare or a pheasant; they might
be sorry when found out and had to suffer for it.

The Tempests, who had a life interest in the Tong estate, had more to fear from other quarters than Pudsey, though it was well known that they were very jealous of some of the Pudsey folks. The influence of the Tempests, who sat on the Bradford bench of magistrates, where all criminals in the locality were charged, fined, imprisoned, or sent to the Sessions or Assizes, was very great, and helped to lower the character of Pudsey as a village in the estimation of such as shared the large landowners' prejudice touching game and the game laws. We confess that though never in the poaching business ourselves, we could never think poaching a crime, except so far as bad laws make good actions illegal. This is not the place to enter into the subject of what we always considered the wicked and pernicious game laws, but we never could imagine it possible for either a Tempest or anyone else to be able to swear to or prove the identity of those wild birds and animals, even when on their own estates, and much less when outside their domain.

But if that could be done, those farmers on adjoining lands ought to have had a claim for compensation against the Tempests for allowing their game to trespass. We repeat that it always appeared to us that the Game Laws—made by rich landowners for their own special gratification, and for the upholding of which the whole community was taxed—made certain actions crimes which were not such, and we insist that in judging the character of Pudsey people by their criminal record, that all cases of poaching should be deducted from Pudsey and added to Tong, or rather to the Tempests. Were poachers charged with trespassing it would be quite another thing, where they had not the consent of the farmers. What dreadful affrays there have been between poachers and keepers, as well as expense to the country in prosecuting and imprisoning men for the special benefit of large landowners! All this will be speedily changed now; for the people having political power will elect men of common sense, lovers of honesty and justice, who will abolish the last remnants of those wicked and unjust game laws.

FETCHING MILK

was very common in our boyhood's days. Very little, if any, was delivered at the people's houses. The custom was to fetch it from farmhouses, and almost everyone fetched the milk they consumed. This milk was mostly called "old," meaning skimmed, that is the cream taken off after standing a day or two. A large amount of buttermilk, called "churned milk," was used. In Tong, Scholebrook, and Tyersal lanes, a large number of boys and girls, and in some cases also men and women, might be seen every morning and evening fetching milk, and frequently very sad accidents would occur in getting along those rough and ugly lanes, when some had the misfortune to stumble and spill their milk, and had to go home and face their family with an empty can, *milkless*. Others fetched their milk from other outside places, east, north, and west of the village, while some got it from persons in the village who kept a cow or two. A large amount of shoe leather (or of clogs) was consumed, as well as time spent by this custom. Old milk was a halfpenny per pint, churnmilk two or three times cheaper than that, as some gave twice as much of it as others did for a penny; while new milk was a penny per pint everywhere the same. New milk was much better then than now; at least we thought it rich then and do not think that much of it is so now. Of course, as in the case of the Fulneck penny pies, some allowance ought probably to be made from the fact of our boyish sense of taste being more acute than it is today. New milk was fifty per cent cheaper than it is now, notwithstanding that the old Corn Laws have been abolished, which Protectionists predicted would ruin the farmers by reducing the price of all farm produce. Now we incline to think that a penny per pint was too little for good unadulterated new milk, but three half-pence (which is half as much more) ought to pay the farmer well, and if kept pure and good we are persuaded that a much larger quantity could be sold than at present.

Our fetching milk from Tong, our "blegging" there—that is, gathering blackberries and sometimes elderberries—or gleaning in the cornfields, with the family relationships we had there, helped to form associations most dear to us, and which after nearly sixty years have never been effaced.

The following may not be deemed strictly within our province in writing on Progress in Pudsey, but what we thought relevant has revived remembrances in which we feel inclined to indulge for a minute or two, hoping that no one will be the worse by our slight digression, if such it may be called.

When a boy, Abee lane, Tong beck and lane, the profusion of hawthorn blossom, wild roses and honeysuckle, with songs of birds as we went along, all combined to make it appear in our eyes a Paradise. And certainly, apart from our childish fancy and possible exaggeration, the scenery then far surpassed what we see today, since the mills close by were erected, and the minerals were being got on the Tong estate, and some of the timber cut down as well. We may be told that our ideas of progress being carried out have spoiled the scenery. But it is not so. For if all the landed estates had been free, land would have got into more hands and been better cultivated; and if tenant farmers had been able to claim for all real improvements made in or on the land, so much labour would have been required in its culture, and so much more wealth produced in the shape of eatables (which we need, but are compelled to get from other countries), that there would not have been that rush to manufacturing enterprises we have seen, and tens of thousands who have been compelled to leave such places as Tong, or been prevented from going there, have overcrowded other villages, towns, and cities, elbowing their fellowmen in mills, factories, and workshops instead of being on the land, breathing a purer air, moving in a more moral atmosphere, and living more happy and prosperous lives. We remark in concluding this article, that when a boy the Tong church bells had a wonderful charm for us. No bells ever rung out such smooth, subdued, sweet, and mellow tones as they did, and we have never heard them since without a peculiar feeling—unlike anything experienced whilst listening to other bells. Probably our early associations have something to do with the matter, and those who lived on the southern part of Pudsey will better appreciate our sentiments than it is possible for those to do who lived on the more distant northern part, and who would be less acquainted with the sound of Tong church bells.

It may not be amiss to state that thirty years ago, in 1856, while sitting alone in our garden in front of our house which stood alone, and at some distance from any other house, so that all was quiet and still, except a gentle summer breeze which wafted the sound of Tong church bells across the woods and vales, which so impressed us, by reviving old memories, that we wrote in pencil on the spot as we sat, the following lines, and a long time after composed a tune for them with piano accompaniment, which however faulty it might be considered by professors of music, gives to the lines the sentiment we attach to them. Both words and music were composed for our own pleasure, which we think is legitimate when it does not interfere with the rights and happiness of anyone else. We may add that as they were for home use only, we dedicated them to our children and grandchildren.

WRITTEN ON LISTENING TO TONG CHURCH BELLS, 1856

Ring ye, sweet Tong bells, as ever,
Chimes that cheered me when a child,
Peals so dear, O may I never
Fail to be by you beguiled.
Yours is no mere noise and clatter—
Chaste your tones, solemn and shrill,
Making it a sacred matter,
Ringing music on the hill.

Ring your peals, so joyful, bringing
Solace to the troubled breast;
Like angelic choirs were singing,
Calling souls to final rest.
In Tong Lane, I well remember,
'Mid entrancing scenery,
In the month of ripe September,
How your song enchanted me!

At the birth of my dear mother
Rang ye peals, and when she wed;
But at times ye ring another,
Far more solemn—for the dead,
Joining in our daily sorrow,
Sharing too our greatest joy—
Dark today, and bright tomorrow—
Life at best hath some alloy.

Your sweet music doth not tarry,
Through the air it rings and swells,
Gentle breezes it doth carry
O'er the woods and lovely dells.
Ring ye, sweet Tong bells, as ever,
Chimes that cheered me when a child;
Peals so dear, O may I never
Fail to be by you beguiled.

CHAPTER XVII

Progress in Music

Ignorance of Music sixty years ago—Prejudice against Organs—
Difficulties in striking tunes at Chapels—A woman comes to the
rescue—Blunders of leading singers and their self-conceit—
Pudsey Old Reed Band—Some droll characters—The Drummer—
All gone!—Shakespeare's lines—Old-time recollections—Music
then and now—Pudsey Choral Union and its numerous patrons—
Influences of Bands of Hope—Services of Song—Our National
system of Education—Pianos then and now—A curious soul with
no taste for music—The universe full of music—What some think
the best thing.

Perhaps there is nothing in which Pudsey has made so much
progress during the last sixty years as it has in music. Very few,
sixty years ago, understood music, or ever heard first-class selections performed. None of the chapels had an organ, except Fulneck, which was quite an exception, as we have previously shown,
being a place where music was taught to pupils from a distance.
We question whether at that day any of the other chapel people
would have had one given, there being much prejudice against
them in most places of worship, and divisions, or splits, were
caused by their introduction in places where they boasted of
being far ahead of Pudsey folks in intelligence. In some of the
chapels might be seen a bass called a *"base,"* which was used as
much as anything to get the right pitch, if it happened to be
properly tuned. Some of the congregations were often without
a leading singer, that is, a man to strike the tunes for them,
when it was left for anyone in the chapel to do that, and we have
often seen the whole business in sad straits on that account.
Some times the minister has tried and succeeded, whilst at other
times he failed, and several in succession have tried, and all
failed, when the hymn had to be dispensed with and one with
a metre substituted that some one knew a tune to suit. At one
Methodist chapel a woman with a beautiful, clear voice, and a
soul full of music, often helped all the rest out of the difficulty
by striking the tunes when she was there, but if she happened
to be absent it was often a bad job. We remember tunes being
pitched either too high or too low, so that when the higher notes
were reached the congregation stuck fast. Some might try to

drop an octave, while at other times, if too low, the result was very much the same, but in the opposite direction, and the singing had to be dispensed with altogether. At some of these places they had what was called a voluntary leading singer, an officer without pay, but he could not or would not always be in the singing pew, and if no base happened to be there, he himself sometimes pitched the tunes on the wrong key. But this man had some self-conceit about him, and knowing he was not looked upon as being very reliable in his profession, on an extra occasion he would be absent to show how important his abilities were, and leave them in the lurch, as he said, and laughed heartily when he found that the congregation had been in difficulties. There was some jealousy amongst a few who knew a little music, each thinking himself superior to the other, and it was a common thing at that day to speak of ringers and singers as a rather self-conceited lot of men, and we hardly wonder at it being so, when so few could either ring or sing scientifically. We should think that a more general knowledge of music, the many organs, harmoniums, efficient leaders and choirs will have cured this, at least we hope so.

We remember the Pudsey Old Reed Band, sixty years ago, and knew every member of it before it broke up. This Band was reckoned famous in its days as a local band. It had its clarionets, trumpets, bugles, trombones, French horns, base horns, serpents, bassoons, fifes, and of course the big drum. And such characters, too, there were in that Old Band. From the leader to the drummer might be found any amount of mirth, wit, humour, and drollery. A man like Charles Dickens would have found ample material for a three-volume novel equal to "Pickwick" amongst the members of the Pudsey Old Reed Band. We have often thought that as a rule, music, mirth, and humour were often found closely allied. Whether it is necessarily so is questionable. But formerly, when a knowledge of music was more limited, we incline to think it was so. We remember seeing the player on the big drum when he was about thirty-two years of age, and considered by the bandsmen unequalled as a timekeeper, and said to be such a help to them when playing in the midst of the noisy march and crowds, in keeping the various instrumentalists well together by his correct beat. Then to see how the band was protected in their performances, especially the drummer, who required much more space than other drummers did, and to this end many men might be seen in blue smocks formed six or eight abreast, arm in arm, behind the drummer, to keep off the pressing crowd of spectators or followers, whilst above the heads of the surging crowd might be seen at times the drummer's right hand with drumstick attached to his fingers by a loop, waving in various fantastic shapes, whilst he beat proper time with his left hand. At other times he might be seen beating time with both hands, first on the left and then on the right end of the drum. People who stood at a distance from the crowd, too far off to distinguish the identity of the person performing, said they could always tell who the drummer was by the flourishing of the right hand drumstick above the heads of the crowd. We knew this drummer well; he had an inexhaustable fund of innocent wit and humour, was industrious, and one of the most honest and upright men ever known. Had he been favoured with a good education, instead of having never been able to go to school, but to work from being a young boy almost day and night, during his apprenticeship only half fed and clad, we have no doubt the world would have known more of him. As it was, he was respected by all who knew him whose opinion was worth anything, and left this world, having done more for it than the world had done for him. Left this world did we say? Yes, and all the original members of that famous band of musicians have long since passed away, and gone to their final resting place. We watched them drop off one by one till none were left. Whilst writing this, and thinking of the various characters which composed the Pudsey Old Band, the words of Hamlet to Horatio have come to our mind. Taking from the gravedigger a skull, which he is told is Yorick's, and holding it up, he says: "Alas, poor Yorick! I knew him, Horatio, a fellow of infinite jest, of most excellent fancy: he hath borne me on his back a thousand times; and now how abhorred my imagination is! My gorge rises at it. There hung those lips that I have kissed I know not how oft." Then, addressing Yorick's skull, he asks: "Where be your gibes now? your gambols? your songs? your flashes of merriment, that were wont to set the table on a roar?"

Since we began to write these chapters we have often found our eyes unconsciously filled with tears, *heart-felt tears*, in our various sketches of old-time customs and doings, where our well-known neighbours, friends, relations, or townsmen, and towns-women, long since gone, have been brought fresh before our minds, but whose names we have not thought fit to mention. Histories, biographies, sayings, doings, and anecdotes innumerable might have been given in connection with what we have written, but would not have been (strictly speaking) to the point in showing the progress Pudsey had made.

After the Old Band came the Fartown Band, or what we may call such, as most of the performers lived in or near that locality, and practised there; in time this Band was considered a rather good one by some. But we must not forget that the music performed in those days was only child's play compared with what is performed at the present time by the Pudsey Choral Union, and the various Bands, etc. We see from the advertisements from time to time in the Pudsey papers, announcing the character of the performances, that a class of music is now performed which the old-time musicians would have deemed impossible. Some of the high-class music was not then composed, while the price of such as was composed would be so high as to have prevented the working men with their then small means procuring it. Then there would have been the cost of an expensive teacher to teach it, and arrange if for the different instruments; and perhaps more than all, the long working hours then customary would have made it impossible for them to have spent sufficient time to execute such difficult selections and compositions.

Sixty years ago there were very few pianos in Pudsey. A few old square or table pianos and harpsichords might be found, but very few indeed. It would be edifying for us to know how many there really were then; and how many pianos, harmoniums, and organs there are today, for we are convinced that this alone would show the progress in Pudsey, as far as these instruments are concerned, to be what almost everyone would think incredible. The fact is the people generally then had seldom if ever seen one, and very few would be able to play one; and long since the time of which we are speaking, we have often heard woollen manufacturers and others, who were well off, and some, too, who spent much more in drink than a hand-loom weaver could earn, say that they would *find their lasses summat better ta du, nor to lake wi' a piano.*"

Since that time there has been such a revolution in the price and variety of musical compositions, as the world had never seen before. They have been sown *broadcast,* and it would be very interesting to know, were it possible, how many pieces of music per head there are now and how many sixty years ago. A general knowledge of music has been diffused amongst all classes in Pudsey during the last twenty or thirty years, and the general education which is being carried on there, will be sure to have that tendency.

The late John Whitley did much directly and indirectly to popularise a higher class of music in Pudsey, as well as in the surrounding locality. And much praise is also due to many others in Pudsey, whose names we forbear to mention, lest in doing so we should seem to make invidious distinctions in leaving out names we might forget, or those of others with whom we are at present unacquainted; but we could mention a few who have spent a life-time in arranging music and teaching and conducting the various bands and orchestras, and others who give promise that they will follow in their steps.

On the 19th of March, 1886, we saw an advertisement in the *Advertiser*, announcing a concert to take place on the 29th, by the Pudsey Choral Union, and from the fact that besides a president the names of fifteen vice-presidents appeared, consisting of some of the leading men in the town, we concluded it would be a success. This showed what a great change had taken place in Pudsey in regard to musical performances within our own knowledge, for the pieces to be performed, too, were of such a class as to force upon our attention the contrast, comparing it with the old-time music once performed by the villagers. The first part was to be Weber's "Mass in G," and the second part Sterndale Bennett's cantata "May Queen." What did the people of Pudsey know about such music fifty years ago, and how many could have executed such pieces? Very few in those days could read any kind of music, but now even the children are having their organs of tune and time developed (as the phrenologist would say), as never before, by singing in connection with Bands of Hope, Services of Song, and choirs singing beautiful melodies put to words teaching principles and lessons which will enoble the young mind, and also be preparing them when further advanced in life to take part in the performance of higher class music.

Now that we have our system of National Education and children can learn reading, writing, and arithmetic, and much more, Sunday schools should be more at liberty to teach moral principles and cultivate music—an innocent and beneficial recreation for the children who have been confined in the day schools during the week, and the older ones maybe in the workshop—and so be made more attractive. Let the children sing to their hearts' content. There is no easier method of instilling rational and moralising principles into the children's minds than singing, by which impressions are made which will last through life, growing into a virtuous and enobling development, proving a blessing to themselves, their parents, and the country at large. For music tends to refine the feelings of the singer, to divert the attention from, and blunt the appetite for, the grovelling allurements spread like so many nets in every direction by those whose tastes are debased.

That man has a curious soul who has no taste for music. A world without music would be a blank to such as have proper feelings and whose nervous system is properly strung. But a world without music is impossible. The universe is full of it. We could not exist without some music or harmony, and to one whose eyes are open, and whose soul is not corrupted by the vices of the age, there is music everywhere—in the sweet and merry songs of birds, the humming of bees, the cooing of the dove, the pattering raindrops, the running brook, the merry voices of children, and in a thousand other objects on every hand. Without music or harmony all is jargon and discord. A right-minded person is unhappy where there is no harmony; it is harmony that makes a happy fireside. "Love at home" means music and harmony there in disposition, voice, and action towards each other. A happy family, neighbourhood, village, town, city, or country means very little discord and much harmony there. This boundless universe could not hang together without harmony. And to teach the human voice how to sing, or to teach a person how to perform music on an instrument, which can only be valuable in proportion as it is capable of imitating a well-tuned human voice, is simply to bring the learner into agreement with the universe and to promote human happiness thereby.

All music is sacred; we pay no attention to those persons who talk about "profane" music; there is no such thing, though there may be profanity in its execution, in being badly done, or in the spirit in which it is performed. As to the words put to music, that is another affair, and may be like all other words, compositions, or books, good, bad, or indifferent.

The hypercritical or vicious, whose whole thoughts have been occupied in the mere animal pursuits of life, in getting gold, or in eating and drinking, or something worse, may laugh at what we are writing on music. But it will only prove that their finer senses, if ever they had any, have been blunted by neglecting their cultivation. If finer senses they never had, then it is the fault of their organisation, and they are more to be pitied than blamed. But be that as it may, it is a great calamity, which deprives them of one of the richest sources of life's enjoyments. In our experience we have met with persons who were never able to see anything better, higher, or more sublime, than a "thumping beefsteak and a quart of ale." They have told us so in plain words, and have proved by their vulgar laugh when higher thoughts and feelings were expressed and manifested by persons of a higher and finer mould, that they had sinned away their day of grace, and were better fitted to furnish food for the worms than they were to enjoy a world like this, where earth, sea, and sky are filled with teeming millions of joyous attractions of which they had no knowledge, and for which they had no relish.

Chapeltown, Pudsey, near Leeds,

July 12th, 1886.

Dear Sir—I scarcely need say with what pleasure I have read your very excellent articles on Pudsey sixty years ago. They are true to the letter, as I well know. In collecting notes on musical matters I had been wondering who could give me a list of the Pudsey Old Band, when lo! your graphic account of the Band appears, true to the life. Will you please to jot down all the names of the Band you can remember, with the names of the instruments on which they performed, and forward the same to me at your earliest convenience.—Yours very truly,

SIMEON RAYNER

CHAPTER XVIII

The Hall of Freedom Project

Thirty-five years ago Pudsey had no large Hall or Lecture Room—Schools and Chapels not accessible for the advocacy of unpopular principles—The Temperance Room—Bad feeling caused by letting it for heterodox principles—Unfairness of orthodox Teetotallers towards heterodox Teetotallers—Barker unable to get a room to lecture on Temperance—Working men sign a pledge and resolve to build a Hall for the advocacy of all creeds and opinions—Extract from the first report—How it all ended.

Thirty-five years ago, Pudsey would have about 12,000 inhabitants, and yet there was no large public Hall, or room for lectures, meetings, concerts, etc. The various religious sects had school-rooms connected with their places of worship, but none of them seemed to think that the affairs of this life had much to do with religion, or that it was right and proper to allow the advocacy of doctrines or principles which were opposed to their respective ways of thinking. One or two of the schools might be got sometimes for temperance lectures if a majority of the trustees were favourable, but even then it was either stipulated or understood that nothing should be advanced by the speakers at such lectures or meetings contrary to the orthodox religion as then taught. It was quite common to ask that the name or names of speakers at such meetings should be furnished before the loan of a school-room could be granted, so that a kind of religious Inquisitions were frequent. We have known cases where much uproar, confusion, and bitterness of feeling were the result of applications made, whether the school-room was granted or refused. Sometimes it happened that a speaker consciously or inadvertently would make use of an expression that was thought heterodox by those who were sound in the faith, and much commotion was the result. Nearly all those who had been Barkerites were teetotallers, but were known to be unbelievers in the prevailing theology, and many of them had been so accustomed to speak on and discuss theological matters that it was very difficult for them to speak on temperance without using some phrase that more or less came in contact disagreeably with the popular creeds. It was a great hardship to such to be kept down, muzzled and embarrassed, by the severe and rigid restrictions under which it was known they had to speak. When chapels or schools were accessible for temperance meetings the mention of both politics and religion was prohibited. This stipulation, however, did not mean that the propagation of the orthodox faith, or the defence of the British Constitution as it then stood, would be an infringement of the conditions on which the place was lent. Hence a condition was frequently made that the meeting should be opened by public prayer by someone known to be sound in the faith, and it was quite common to hear orthodox temperance men crowd into their prayers and speeches as much theology as they could. They would talk and pray about the Triune God, the Blessed Trinity, the Expiatory Death of Christ, the Atoning Blood of the Lamb, total Birth Depravity in consequence of Adam's Fall, the Intercession of Jesus and His Godhead, Salvation by Faith alone, and the utter worthlessness of all good works, the literal never-ending flames of hell, and a personal devil, etc.

Some of these orthodox temperance prayers and speakers seemed to go out of their way to have a hit at the Barkerite and Unitarian teetotallers, knowing that the latter were heavily handicapped by not being allowed to open their lips to reply in self-defence. Whereas the heterodox speakers were as conscientious as the orthodox, they had strong convictions of their own, and felt themselves unfairly dealt with. To the credit of some of the better class of orthodox religionists be it said that they strongly condemned the conduct of those of their own creed for the cowardly way in which they acted towards such as differed from them in opinion, and maintained that both in prayer and speech everything should be avoided tending to give offence to those whose lips were sealed upon religious matters. Then the Barkerites had ransacked the Old and New Testaments, and were good Scriptarians, as before stated, and had come to the conclusion that public prayer was un-Christian. They thought that Jesus condemned it both in His teaching and practice, especially when he said in St. Matthew's gospel, chapter 6, verses 5 and 6, as follows:—

"And when thou prayest thou shalt not be as the hypocrites are; for they love to pray standing in the synagogue [Jewish chapel] and in the corners of the streets, that they may be seen of men. Verily I say unto you, they have their reward. But thou when thou prayest enter into thy closet, and when thou hast shut the door, pray to thy Father which is in secret; and thy Father which seeth in secret will reward thee openly."

Now to compel such men to pray in public (had they been allowed) as a condition of having the loan of a place to speak in, appeared to them arbitrary; and to be compelled to listen to so much in the prayers and speeches of others which they looked upon as little less than blasphemous, while they were forbidden uttering one single word of doubt in relation to such matters, made their speaking irksome and unpleasant. Yes, only thirty-five years ago there were many in Pudsey who appeared to think the heavens would fall if opinions contrary to their own were allowed to be propagated. They had no idea that others had as much right to their own opinions as they had to theirs.

The well-known Joseph Barker was a great teetotaller and popular advocate of temperance principles, but after he was expelled by the Conference for not being orthodox, none of the religious sects would allow him to speak in their chapels or school-rooms. Very few of the Temperance Halls, which had been built for the purpose of advocating temperance principles, could be got for him to speak in, and for differing in opinion on religion from many of the teetotallers his advocacy of temperance was refused. Many teetotal societies were broken up, and others nearly so, by the perpetual interference with men's theological opinions. It was the same to a large extent with regard to politics. A thorough Radical, and especially a Republican, was not allowed to speak in any of the chapels and schools. The Pudsey Temperance Society hired a small room at various times in different localities, which was mostly an upper room in a chamber formerly occupied by hand-loom weavers. Such were most accessible for lectures on unpopular isms, though even these rooms could seldom be got without much animosity and strong opposition on the part of those anti-reformers. Subscriptions to the temperance cause were frequently stopped because the room had been let for the advocacy of theological or political heresy.

Probably some who read the above remarks may be wondering what we mean by the foregoing, and may be unable to see what bearing they can have upon our heading, "The Hall of Freedom Project." This, however, we will now try to show.

In 1851 there was a large number of persons in Pudsey who did not think that either the popular theology or popular politics were perfect. While there were others who thought it best to let "truth and falsehood grapple," believing that the result would be a victory for the former. A few of these men happened to be met together in January, 1851, talking about the difficulties long felt in not having a large Hall for lectures, public meetings, etc. These few men drew up a pledge and signed it, resolving never to rest satisfied till a large room or Hall was erected, to be let on reasonable terms to all sects and parties for the advocacy of every kind of ism, and for public meetings, concerts, balls, festivals, panoramas, dioramas, etc. Bills were written and posted calling a public meeting of the inhabitants, and setting forth the objects of the same. A number of working men answered the call, and it was resolved to build a Hall to cost one thousand pounds, by shares of one pound each, to be paid for when opened so as not to be hampered by a mortgage debt, and that it should be called "The Hall of Freedom." A prospectus was drawn up and circulated; the town divided into districts and canvassed for shareholders; a committee was formed with a president, treasurer, and secretary; collectors were appointed to collect the weekly subscriptions from shareholders, all monies thus collected to be deposited in the Leeds Building Society, called "The Provincial Benefit Building Society."

It may not be out of place here to give a few extracts from the Secretary's first report now lying before us, which was read to a crowded meeting of shareholders and their wives, after a meat tea, in the Temperance Room, Greenside. It will show to some extent the spirit of the time, and the enthusiasm of the promoters of the projected Hall of Freedom.

The report states that there were 270 shareholders, that £243 13s. 6d. had been collected, and deposited in the Building Society mentioned before.

The total expenses of floating the concern in printing, stationery, meetings, etc., had only been £4 5s. 8d. Many of the shareholders had promised to increase their shares, while many persons who had previously stood aloof promised to take up shares, seeing it was going to be a success. Probably a more energetic lot of men were never known than the principal workers on behalf of the Hall of Freedom—none of whom received a single penny of pay either for labour or personal expenses, and many interesting anecdotes might be told in connection with the project. A friend of mine has just told me one which shows the eagerness displayed in getting shareholders, though we cannot defend the means our friend adopted to get a certain friend of his (who had been frequently urged to do so but without success) to take up a share. This friend of ours was in the habit of mesmerising his friend, who was a very industrious and temperate person, and had money put by for a "rainy day." One evening, while the latter personage was in a mesmeric state, our friend after touching the organ of benevolence asked him to take a few shares in the Hall of Freedom, and he immediately offered all his money and would have taken up all the shares untaken had he been heeded. After being put into his natural state, and informed as to what he had done, he was not well satisfied with the transaction. This young man was known to be very miserly, and there was no chance of his giving much to anything except when mesmerised. We have known many well able to help a good cause, but not willing to do so, and know of no means of getting assistance from such for purposes of public utility except some larger-hearted friend could succeed in mesmerising them, and though we cannot recommend the operation, it is certain they deserve it.

From the first report before referred to, it appears there had been many excuses made by persons for not taking shares. Some objected because all kinds of creeds were to have an equal chance on the Hall of Freedom platform. There were some great Free Traders who did not believe in Free Speech, but the Hall of Freedom was to be equally accessible to Catholics, Protestants, and to Methodists both old and new; to Baptists, Presbyterians, and Independents; to Calvinists, Armenians, Unitarians, Quakers, Swedenborgians, and Latter-day Saints; to Jews, Mohammedans, and Hindoos; or to persons who might differ from all of them. It was to be let to Whigs, Tories, Radicals, Chartists, or Republicans; for public meetings, concerts, or balls. The advantage is shown of being able to hold public meetings where the inhabitants would have an opportunity of expressing their opinions on all the current and prominent topics of the day, which up to that time they never had. The only places for town's meetings were either the church vestry or a large room at the workhouse, Littlemoor, and when too small to accommodate all present an adjournment was made to the open air. The report goes on to state that from the commencement there had been the greatest unanimity amongst both the workers and the shareholders. The need of a large public hall is then shown from the fact of the universal agitations for a larger share of freedom, the general breaking up of old worn-out institutions, and the worldwide struggle for liberty against slavery and oppression. From Cape Horn to the Canadas there was general commotion. In various parts of South America there was perpetual insurrection and rebellion. Cuba in the West Indies was struggling to throw off the Spanish yoke; more than three millions of negroes in the American Slave States were in bondage; but such an agitation was going on against slavery as was never known before. Harriet Beecher Stowe had written her "Uncle Tom's Cabin," and electrified the whole civilised world by revealing the horrors of that fiendish system. Lloyd Garrison was thundering forth by his abolition speeches and his press; and Theodore Parker, and Wendell Phillips, of Boston, and Doctor Furniss, of Philadelphia, Burleigh, Burr, and Wright, with hundreds more, were denouncing the doctrine of the "Rights of property in man;" whilst

Frederick Douglas represented and defended his race—the negroes—from the base calumnies heaped upon it. Then came Canada for reforms and her struggles to throw off British rule there. The eastern hemisphere was said to have been no less disturbed than the western. From the Cape of Good Hope to St. Petersburg all was turmoil. The Caffres were struggling for their rights, while the negroes were running away from America's boasted land of liberty to form a republic of their own in Liberia in Western Africa. Italy, with her clear skies but insulted people, no longer believed in what the Pope said. There was Austria with her inhuman Haynaus trampling on the liberties of the poor peacable Hungarians, imprisoning and torturing hundreds of her noble Kossuths. While in Ireland there was perpetual hate of the Union forced upon them without their consent, and where English laws had to be enforced at the point of foreign bayonets. In England the people had no *real* political power, but were unmercifully taxed to supply their oppressors with the power of oppressing them. There was much talk about reform in England, but it all ended in talk, and very little desire was manifested to do full justice to the people. When the Hall of Freedom was opened the people of Pudsey would be able to meet together in large numbers to hear lectures and help to form public opinion, not only to be heard at St. Stephen's, but in other lands, where the oppressed in all nations might be *fraternised* with, and the tyrannies throughout the world in every shape and form by public exposure be shamed out of existence.

The above brief abstract of the first report shows that there were persons in Pudsey thirty-five years ago, who took note of public events and had their eyes open to the wrongs of oppressed peoples, and were anxious and willing to do something towards helping truth and justice both in our own and other lands, having strong hopes and aspirations with regard to the final triumph of *right* over *might*.

After a while the Hall of Freedom committee were informed that the Lowtown Methodists needed more Sunday school accommodation, and that they were going to erect one much larger on purpose to let it for lectures and public meetings at a reasonable rate, and to let it to all parties, without restrictions as to creeds. It was said that the projected Hall of Freedom had suggested it, and that it was done to some extent in opposition, as many both chapels, churches, and schools have been, on sectarian principles, to keep other sects and creeds out of certain localities. Be that as it may, many of the shareholders in the Hall of Freedom believed their object would be attained by the erection of the large school-room which was to be called, we believe, the

"Public Room." Others had not faith in the town's wants being met by such room and wished to go on with the Hall project. A meeting of shareholders was called, as it was found difficult to persuade persons to take up additional shares as promised, since the Public Room was to be built, and a majority decided to wind up the affair; which was done, and each subscriber had his or her monies returned.

The Public Room was completed, and we are happy to state that the promoters of the Hall of Freedom had reason to be fairly satisfied with the liberality shown by those who had the letting of it. Pudsey people for the first time were able to meet in large numbers. Since then the splendid building for the Mechanics' Institute has been erected, with its large Lecture Hall, and the town is now well accommodated for holding meetings, etc. Our own opinion is this: had not the Hall of Freedom been projected and promised to be a speedy success, Pudsey would not have had the Public Room erected at the time it was, as an *impetus* was given to it, public attention being aroused to the long felt want and need of a large Lecture Hall. Much good has resulted to the inhabitants by the erection of the Public Room and Victoria Hall, and now that Pudsey is the centre of a Parliamentary Division, returning a member to Parliament by household suffrage too, the use of these large Lecture Halls for public meetings will prove of inestimable value.

CHAPTER XIX

Progress in the Future

The centralisation of business, and the causes—Competition tends to destroy itself—Property has its duties—No two men have the same chances, and why—All cannot be employers of labour—Nor be millionaires—Much better times possible in the future—Why should there be any poverty—The great struggle between labour and capital—Social and political Grievances in the future—New political era—Canon Percival on competition—Vicar of South Cave on pauperism—Man as a savage and as a co-operator.

We concluded Chapter XIV by saying that the woollen business, like all others, was getting into fewer hands—the hands of large capitalists; and that it is so few will deny. Where are all the once small woollen manufacturers of Pudsey? Whole families whose names appeared in old Directories are now either all, or most of them, left out; not that they or their offspring have all died out, but because they have had to succumb to the onward march of progress, unable to hold their own amid the changes that have taken place. This is nothing new or uncommon, for trade and commerce, as carried on hitherto, are very uncertain; there are so many possible risks and disasters besetting them—changes in the prices of the raw material, in styles of goods, and consequent depreciation of stocks, changes in the fiscal policies of foreign nations where our goods are sold, and many other things over which manufacturers and merchants have no control. There is also another remarkable fact, viz., that there are very few men who accumulate wealth whose children's children make it more. The great majority make it less, or perhaps spend it all, and what took the grandfather so much toil and struggling to acquire is mostly spent by the first, second, or at least the third generation. Wealth in many cases seems to have a debilitating effect on those who get it by no efforts of their own. Men who make money, as a rule, best know its value, while those who have it made to their hand are apt to be too proud to carry on business, and act as if their money would never be done. We have sometimes thought that the English aristocracy knew this, and therefore had surrounded their large possessions with such laws as would keep them in their families in spite of the possible incapacity of the possessors, not having confidence in their offsprings' ability to keep it unless safeguarded as personal property cannot be.

As before intimated, many of the once small woollen manufacturers in Pudsey and their descendants have ceased to be such. There are also fewer middlemen, such as oil, ware, listing, and waste dealers, as well as woolstaplers. Most of the manufacturers now go to the fountain head for all they want, and the small profits now realised would not pay middlemen unless the business done was a large one. A man now would find it difficult after saving £20 to begin making woollen cloths, and make it pay as he once could, when he merely spent his money in wool, and readily got mungo, ware, oil, listing, scribbling, warp, and weft delivered at home, all on credit till he was able to sell the cloth and pay for all out of it; or it might be buy more wool with the money, making a still larger lot before paying for the first. Of course such an one would probably have to pay more for articles he got on credit, by many pounds, than what an extensive manufacturer, who had his own machinery and bought everything at first hand, would pay; so that whilst most of the former class would in time lose their all, the latter would probably be getting rich.

Business, we repeat, of all kinds, both woollen, worsted, cotton, boot and shoe, as well as tailoring and the iron business, is getting into fewer hands; and the greater perfection attained in machinery, the more difficult will it be for men of small means to rise in the world as manufacturers, except some other agency should come into operation by which people with small means can hit upon some plan or system whereby they can employ themselves and enjoy what they produce. Though business is becoming more centralised, we maintain that the masses of the people are better off. This may seem to some a self-contradiction, but we think it is not. Our meaning is this: The bulk of the people in Pudsey and elsewhere are better housed, better fed and clothed, can earn more money, and get more of the necessaries of life with what they earn, and can save more than formerly. We are not speaking of the large numbers who are paupers, and others who are always on the verge of pauperism (who in the present state of our so-called civilisation, a really unnatural or artificial state of society, always will exist in spite of the vast increase of the wealth of England and the world), but of the bulk of the working classes.

Civilisation creates wealth, but it also creates new wants and needs; so that the wage earning people of today feel as poor as their class ever did, and are so in relation to the higher standard of living erected of present wants and needs. As an illustration:

Many working people whose incomes are not large must now have a trip to the seaside at least once a year, and many of them also stay a few days there. Whereas formerly if half a dozen weavers and their wives joined together and hired a rough and uneasy conveyance to go to Ilkley and back on the Sunday it served them to talk about during the remainder of their lives. People now produce a larger amount of wealth and get more for it, but do not get as large a proportion of what they produce as formerly. Hence the few get richer, while the many get relatively poorer, compared with the huge mountains of wealth now produced, and the high standard of the necessaries and comforts of life; and hence the widespread discontent and dissatisfaction amongst the labourers, the strikes, Trades Unions, the tendency to Co-operation, and even Socialism, the gigantic struggle betwixt labour and capital.

Competition may be good for a time, in the absence of something better, and is the unavoidable outcome of the ignorance of society, the only thing possible; but it is a hard and cruel schoolmaster to bring society to something more rational and humane under which it is possible for all worthy citizens to avoid being driven to the wall for no fault of their own. It is impossible to prevent poverty in a competitive state of society. Thousands of willing workers in the best of times are without work, owing to our bad arrangements. Why should men have to humble themselves by seeking work? To ask a fellow-mortal to allow them to live or starve? Starvation or the poorhouse is the only alternative of no one being found able or willing to employ them.

There is a notion common among both Free Traders and Protectionists that England has a right to expect the increase of her exports indefinitely, we suppose for ever. We do not see it either probable or possible. On the contrary, England even with universal Free Trade has no right to expect increasing the exports of her manufactured produce for all time to come. Free Trade is most in accordance with sound common sense, favourable to peace and good feeling towards all the world; best from even a rational selfish view, or reviewed in the light of political economy. Free Trade throughout the world is certain to take place as the nations grow wiser, when every man in every clime will be at liberty to produce any article he likes and to sell it to any other man upon earth willing to buy it, without let or hindrance, providing such article is not deemed hurtful in itself and mischievous to mankind. Yet even if such a state of things should take place in 1887, which it will not, England would not reap the advantage from it which some suppose. What right have we to expect being able to beat every other nation in the world in making either locomotives or other engines, machinery, iron or steel rails, woollen, worsted, or cotton goods? Every other nation is being educated, some of them more highly than we, in the various trades; though we are happy to say that England after generations of neglect is now beginning in good earnest to make rapid advances, but we shall do well to hold our own in the general march of progress. We have no objection to England being at the head—our desires lean in that direction; but we have no right to allow our desires or feelings to blind us to patent facts. Australia produces immense quantities of wool; what can hinder that colony from making it up to supply the wants of the colonists, and in time being large exporters of cloths as well? It is the same with regard to America and the cotton business, as well as India and the Cape. The same remarks apply to some extent to our iron trade. We have no reason to expect the old state of things with regard to foreign demands for English goods going on increasing. There is a probability of a few fresh fields being opened out in Africa, and a few other places, where we shall do well if we can get our share without monopolising it all; but it is reasonable to suppose that even those peoples in time will produce their own to a large extent, as skill and intelligence travel more rapidly from clime to clime now than formerly.

The fact is, by our bad legislation an artificial state of things has been produced in England; the people have been driven off and kept from the land, and its cultivation, so that we have been too much dependent on foreign nations for what we could have produced ourselves, and too much dependent on the same taking what we produce in the shape of manufactured goods. Every writer of note, and the bulk of our legislators, are beginning to recognise the most important fact, that the old feudal land laws must be abolished, and the cultivation of land made compulsory. Land is unlike any other commodity. No article can be made without land, our very existence depends upon it; hence special laws are required in relation to it, such as do not apply to any other article. In the times of panics, famines, and other national disasters, when starvation stares tens of thousands in the face, the aristocracy wriggle and twist in every possible manner and form to divert the people's attention from the main cause of suffering, by recommending emigration, taxation of imports, or fresh wars to rob peoples of their countries for the sake of extending our trade and getting fresh customers. The abolition of our bad land laws, and the enacting of rational and just ones, would injure no one, while the whole community would be benefited and the country enriched. Under proper laws we should not need to be either such large importers or exporters, and one thing is certain, that we have nearly got to the end of our folly. Something will have to be done, not only for Ireland and the Crofters but for every other part of the United Kingdom, for though under a false state of things it may be possible for a people to pile up mountains of wealth, it cannot last for ever, and the disparity created between labour and capital will ultimately crush the whole system.

England, under the best of systems, would probably both import and export considerably, exchanging manufactured goods for other articles which our climate cannot produce. But we need more butter, eggs, lard, honey, beef, mutton, pork, and cheese, as well as fruits, vegetables, and poultry, all of which or most of them we could produce ourselves. Why not produce them? In doing which we should require the labour that now *starves*! The land cries, "Give me toil and tillage, and I will show you what I can do." The half starved agricultural labourer and unemployed artizan answer, "I wish I could, am willing, but am not allowed."

The inevitable result of all this *centralisation of wealth in few hands* on the one hand, and the monopoly of land on the other, will be this: the masses have now much political power and will soon have more; when the rich cease to have duplicate votes, when election expenses are reduced, and are paid by the people, and Members of Parliament are paid for their services, so that men who are able, but too poor to devote their time for the people's good without pay, may be elected; when we have manhood and woman suffrage, a rational and just system of registering the claims of voters, when Ireland is allowed a Parliament to manage Irish affairs in the place of the present mock and disgraceful paper Union, and consequent perpetual coercion force, bitterness and hatred, which has proved for the last eighty-five years a curse both to England and Ireland in a hundred different ways, and lowered the former in the estimation of every civilised nation in the world, when the Tory House of Lords is abolished, *all of which are sure to come to pass before long*, for the people are being so rapidly educated both in elementary knowledge and in social and political science, that they will make use of their political power to effect a peacable revolution by legislation, as well as by other social agencies. Governing this country in olden times was done for the most part by *trickery* and *fraud*. With most legislators anything in politics was deemed fair, until it became a proverb. There was no moral conviction, or sense of right or wrong in the matter; we speak of the majority of the old rulers, and not of the exceptions. To be sure they would talk of "England's glory" and go in for "the country's good," but the people at last have found out that "England's glory" meant the rulers' glory in their monopoly of offices, places, pensions, and privileges, and that they took good care to have much more than their share of the "good of the country." Now that the people whose interests have been betrayed have power, it will be quite easy for them to have recourse to equity, to political justice, because they have not only a keener moral sense in politics, but their own interests are linked with justice to all, and have everything to gain and nothing to lose by their action. The rights of property till now have swamped almost every other consideration. We have heard much about even the "sacred rights of property," but seldom heard anything in politics about property having sacred duties. We remember once hearing Sir Wilfrid Lawson speak in the Leeds Town Hall when it was crowded in every part. During his speech he raised his voice to a higher key and said "England is the finest country upon earth," when his utterance was cut short by overwhelming applause. When all was quiet he finished his sentence, which was "for a rich man to live in," it being followed by loud laughter; and so it is. It will be found by comparing the position of wealthy men in England with any others of the same class in any of the great nations on earth, that those who in times past made our laws took special care of themselves.

In addition to improved legislation there will be other social means brought into operation. Co-operation has made rapid strides in distributing wealth; but many large societies have money they hardly know what to do with. Why not invest it in co-operative production? Why not try to produce many articles they sell? Co-operation in the future will be one of the greatest levers in the people's interest. As before stated, men find it impossible now to begin business as once with a small capital, but a thousand men with ten pounds each can raise a capital of ten thousand pounds, and employ labour in farming and manufacturing, and pay a fair share of the wealth produced to the labourers. Large capitalists too will do well to give those they employ an interest in the profits. Competition has its bright features, we say, under a certain state of things—in times of ignorance; but, like all other evils, it contains within itself the seeds of its own destruction; and one thing is certain, that unlimited progress in the future is impossible on the old lines. In competition the few get the largest share, while co-operation confers on all a more equal share.

Some who have been successful in business tell us that everyone has the same chance they have had. But nothing could be more fallacious. There never were two men alike, having the same countenances, or the same views of everything, or the same capabilities for the same vocation. In many cases no two merchants or manufacturers could have the same customers, and it frequently happens that one thrives by getting another man's custom, from numerous causes apart from the superiority of one man over the other. It is impossible for all to be millionaires: there is not wealth enough in the world for that. All men cannot be employers, as there would be no one left to employ except each employed himself only, in which case they would never be very rich if they saved all they earned. No, the competitive system is a sort of gambling, in which the man that fails to make money is not necessarily the worst man, but may have many hindrances and misfortunes that he who got rich had not. He may not have had as good health, or his wife or children might not; he might have had a large family or an extravagant wife, and the other not, or have made bad debts which the other escaped, and a hundred other causes may have operated. How can it be expected that a man who starts with nothing but his labour, uneducated and brought up in the low quarters of a city, can, as a rule, stand the same chance as one well schooled and taught a profitable business his father had established, leaving that son the connection and all his capital? Thousands of men who are wealthy are no better men, in what makes an honourable citizen and a good character, than thousands who live and die poor and unnoticed. And we again ask: Why should there be poverty in a rich world like this? Poverty is bred by society, the result of ignorance and bad social arrangements. Why should a man (we repeat it) have to seek work? This earth might be made to blossom as the rose, and the fact that there are so many paupers and so many on the brink of pauperism, proves the people to be *blockheads* who do not know how to make a proper use of this earth, teeming with every material blessing.

We may be asked what all this has to do with Progress in Pudsey during the last sixty years. It has this to do with it: We do not wish either Pudsey people or any other people to be content with their present condition, much better though it may be than that of their forefathers. After all the advances and improvements made, the condition of the working classes is one of absolute serfdom compared with what it ought to be. We want the people to look up, aim higher, to study social and political problems, and help themselves with their own hands and brains. There are far better times to come than the best we've ever had. We do not say "all aim at being rich," but to be free from poverty and the fear of it, and then in reality you will be rich in the truest sense. There would not be such elbowing each other in society to be rich were there no fear of future want. We read of a very suitable prayer once being made; the petitioner neither wanted poverty nor riches, thinking both extremes bad. Help to crush that most horrible and infamous notion once held by all, and still by some, especially the rich, that it is ordained by Providence that there should be rich and poor in the world. Every right-minded man would rejoice to see a state of things in which every man, woman, and child had all the comforts of life.

Whilst writing the above remarks a large meeting was being held by the unemployed in Trafalgar Square, London, and riots and much destruction of property were the result. This is the natural offspring of our artificial state of society, our bad social arrangement, and political blundering; so are all Trades Unions, strikes, and lock-outs. There is bread in abundance without robbing a man or any set of men, if society was not blinded by ignorance and prejudice. It does not require the thousandth part of the high culture possessed by Mr. Gladstone and Lord Salisbury to destroy much of the poverty by good legislation. All cannot be done in a day nor a year. We are glad to see the noble efforts made in the right direction by the former gentleman, and if he had been faithfully backed up by all those who pretend to be the people's friends he would have done more; and if he lives long enough he will do much good yet. But we think that there are thousands of the better class of artizans connected with Trades' Unions and Co-operative undertakings who, if 670 of them were but in Parliament, would so manage matters, and in a short time so improve the state of society, that the millions would be astonished; and all, too, without doing the slightest injustice to anyone. There is one thing they would soon do, viz., give the people the power over the public drinkshops. We have made drunkards, criminals, and paupers wholesale by licensing public drinkshops. Hundreds of thousands have lived and died criminals, paupers, and beggars who would have been respectable citizens but for the wholesale temptations scattered throughout the country, like so many snares to entrap the weak and unwary. As before said, property also has been treated as if it had no duties attached to it. The only cry has been the "rights of property," and seldom have its obligations been mentioned. This subject, however, is too large to treat at length here, though it is one which every year will be more talked about, agitated, and understood till the time comes, as come it will, when people will wonder at the stupidity and ignorance of past generations in not knowing how to prevent poverty, whilst in possession of such boundless wealth and unlimited resources.

Our present poor-law system will have to be remodelled, which breeds pauperism, and can never cure it. As the Vicar of South-Cave says in a letter to the *Leeds Mercury*, today, August 28th, 1886:—"In England the richest country in the world, one in every thirty-one of our countrymen are paupers. Eight millions per annum are paid in poor rates, besides all the private charities. One-hundred-and-one persons in one year die of starvation in London, the richest city in the world, and yet we neither cure, nor aim at curing, pauperism. Surely some wiser and better system might be devised by which pauperism might be made more self-supporting. See what has been done in London alone by the Jews, in helping their poor to help themselves and also what this Vicar tells us has been done by the Elberfeld plan in reducing pauperism.

Then we *breed* criminals as well as punish actions which are not crimes by our class-made laws; we do not aim so much at curing criminals as punishing them. We allow crime to be a heavy tax upon society when it could be made self-supporting. We have made aggressive wars by which the people's blood has been spilt like water, and their backs been burdened with heavy taxation. All this in the future will be changed. We shall still have progress, and probably more rapid than in the past, but not on the same lines. In fact, already progress is being made on new lines; the struggle between labour and capital becomes more severe, hence the numerous strikes and lock-outs. This state of things will evolve new conditions and relationships, forming new lines and modifying the old. Associations and combinations amongst the producers of wealth—the toilers—have been developed, as seen in the many co-operative undertakings. Our system of National Education will foster and ripen all such projects. Middlemen as distributors, etc., will be more and more dispensed with, and the producers of wealth have a larger share of what they produce.

Never before were the people of this country so wide awake as to the vast importance of land and the land question. The agricultural labourers of England are uniting for land law reform, and so are the tenant-farmers. It is the same in Wales, and in Scotland, and the world knows what a vital question this is in Ireland. Large owners also, convinced at last that something must be done to stave off reform by Parliament, touching the land, are purchasing large landed estates to divide into smaller allotments.

Never before had we such a House of Commons as now for showing its readiness to rectify not only old grievances touching land but other property as well. Compensation for improvements not only in land, but house property also, is entertained; and even our local boards and the promised reform in County Government all prove that general attention is directed to the *duties* of property. The morning after Mr. Crilly introduced his Bill for enabling tenants of town houses in Ireland to obtain compensation for improvements made, the London Correspondent of the *Leeds Mercury* said: "The House of Commons gave a striking proof yesterday that it is prepared to legislate on the question of property in a far more thorough spirit than any of its predecessors"; and that it was clear that it was prepared to legislate on questions affecting landlords and tenants with more regard to the interests of the tenants and the justice of the case than it had ever been before. From one mode or system is evolved another. The old pack-horse, the stage coach, the one-spindled wheel and hand carding, the jenny and hand-loom, all contributed their share to progress; but they have had their day, and better modes have taken their places. So also individual interests in the competitive state have done much good and increased national wealth, but never cured poverty, and never will. The union of wealth producers by co-operative undertakings must take the place of "everyone for himself," so as to secure the better distribution of life's comforts to the exclusion of none willing to lend their brain, skill, and muscle for the common good of all.

Since writing the above we were agreeably surprised to find such a strong condemnation of the present competitive state of society in a sermon preached in St. Andrew's Parish Church, Plymouth, on Sunday, June 13th, by the Rev. J. Percival, M.A., Canon of Bristol, before the members of the Co-operative Congress, assembled at Plymouth this year. Amongst other equally strong remarks we find the following: "Competition is neither more or less than the expression in our social activity of individual selfishness. However we wrap it up and disguise its character, when we come to examine it, we find that it is at bottom nothing else but the endeavour to make gain for ourselves out of the struggle for individual success. It is in fact a sort of strife or warfare. . . . In competition, then, you see the last phase of the never-ending battle of selfish instincts, and in plain language that motto which might be written all over it as its best description is "the weakest to the wall." . . . Then he asks: "Are we to accept this ruling principle of competition as a natural and unchangeable law of human society? Is this veiled warfare between man and man, with whose laws and customs the strong manufacturer or the wealthy tradesman may buy up, or undersell, or ruin the smaller man, and then having secured his monopoly may proceed to reap his harvest? Is this gospel of brute force, directed by selfish intelligence, always to hold the field of social life, and to give to men's daily occupations, thoughts, and aims, their prevailing character? Must we acquiesce in this as an eradicable part of our social system? These are the questions men are asking more and more persistently every year, and I put them to you very plainly because they lie behind and underneath every other question about the improvement of our common life; and your answer to such questions as these will depend upon your ideas of what Christianity is and is to be in our life and society. Do you say then that this competition, which sets one man against another in every trade and every industry, is unchangeable and right, that it is inherent in our life, and that we must be content simply to make the best of it?"

We find that man, from being a mere animal—in a savage state, living on wild fruits and roots, or hunting and fishing, struggling for existence with very little aid beyond his finger nails and teeth—then joins his fellows, who move in tribes, tribe contending with tribe; prisoners of war are made slaves to toil and plod for their captors, others are stolen, or bred, bought and sold like cattle. Sometimes we see men under feudalism, where they are sold and transferred with the soil. In course of time man gets his freedom, and begins to struggle for the largest share of the earth, and the products of other men's labour. From fear of future want, or from personal ambition or greed, the struggle becomes severe; the strongest, most cunning, or what are called "the fittest," survive, though by no means the most deserving, tried by a moral standard. Men are at their wits' end to invent and discover new modes of acquiring riches; wealth increases, so that the granaries and warehouses groan beneath the weight of the luxuries and necessaries of life, but the largest share is owned by the few, while tens of thousands are in want of the necessaries of life. In time the people are educated, are enlightened, become less animal and more refined, have higher aims and aspirations. The old standard of living is despised, and some of the wisest and largest hearted discover the blunders in society's present arrangements, and appeal to the people. They say: "Brothers in toil—let us join hands. Let us cease to elbow each other. Let us make it possible to love our neighbours as ourselves. The world is made rich by labour, let us unite together for our mutual interests, that we may destroy poverty and the fear of it; let us help ourselves by helping one another, without injuring anyone else," and the people in time say "Amen."

While we could extend our trade we managed to get along somehow. There is a limit to this extension. With our bad land laws, we should have stuck fast generations ago but for our large foreign trade; and if the old corn laws had not been abolished we should have had either reform or revolution long before now. Depressed trade cannot be the result of over-population, because there is enough for all if they could get it. Nor can the cause be over-production so long as what is produced is needed by men willing to toil.

It is the duty of all to unite as one man not merely to relieve poverty by charity, but to aim at preventing poverty, and to cure it where it exists. It is the interest of even the wealthy people that poverty should be destroyed, and that every decent man and woman should be delivered from the fear of future want. We hope the people of Pudsey will not be behind in laying hold of the new lines of progress, and that during the next fifty or sixty years they may keep in step in the general march of improvement.

CHAPTER XX

Concluding Chapter

Our object in the previous chapters—Great fault of historians—
Macaulay comes to the rescue—Old-time manners and customs
passing away—A friendly letter and the "Plug Riots"—Mayhall—
Extracts from a Biography—Our critics—A postcard from an
unknown writer—Fulneck—The Encyclopaedia Britannica—
Baines' Directory—The writer of postal not "posted"—Pudsey
might and ought to have made more progress during the last
sixty years—We hope and expect better things in the future.

In the foregoing chapters we have neither tried to please or grieve
any class of persons but have aimed at representing Pudsey and
its people as we have seen them in former days; so that the
young folks living today might be able to judge of the progress
made, by comparing one with the other. It was not our purpose
to give statistics relating to the present number of places of
worship, schools, and the average attendance; or the present
rateable value and assessment of rates; its present and proposed
railway facilities, etc. Those who feel interested in the subject
can at any time get such information for themselves. But should
what we have written be preserved by appearing in book form,
as many have urged us to allow, every year that rolls round will
add to its importance; and possibly, as a friendly critic said some
time since in a letter to the *Advertiser*, "furnish the future historian with some material for real history."

One serious fault in most of the histories we read when young,
and which deeply impressed us at the time, was the everlasting
scribble about the kings and queens, nobles and dukes, generals
and their great feats in various battles, and the consequent
wholesale suffering, murder, and death. There was very little
about the large masses of the people—what they were thinking,
doing, and suffering. Of course, royal personages and the aristocracy managed or mismanaged all national affairs, and the rest
were political serfs of whom few historians deemed it worth their
while to take any notice. Imagine therefore our unbounded relief
and pleasure when is America, in the year 1849, we got the first
volume of Macaulay's History of England, published by Harper
Brothers of New York, and read on the first page the following

passage—on the margin of which we immediately wrote in phonography "very good":—

"I should very imperfectly execute the task which I have undertaken if I were merely to treat of battles and sieges, of the rise and fall of Administrations, of intrigue in the palace, and of debates in Parliament. It will be my endeavour to relate the history of the people, as well as the history of the government, to trace the progress of useful and ornamental arts, to describe the rise of religious sects and the changes of literary taste, to portray the manners of successive generations, and not to pass by with neglect even the revolutions which have taken place in dress, furniture, repasts, and public amusements. I shall cheerfully bear the reproach of having descended below the dignity of history if I can succeed in placing before the English of the nineteenth century a true picture of their ancestors."

This passage came as a light to cheer us; there was henceforth hopes of being delivered from the old historical darkness and thraldom, for we always wanted to know what the people were doing.

Many of the old-time habits, manners, and customs of Pudsey are passing away, whilst others are almost forgotten. Those which are foolish and hurtful we hope the young people will help to demolish, and substitute others more in accordance with our advancing civilisation. It is certain that progress in the future will go on, and, as we think has been said by us before, fifty years hence much of what we at present boast, will then be looked upon as rude and barbarous.

Much more might easily have been written on our subject, but we wished to be as brief as possible in giving a general sketch of Pudsey life, and have found some difficulty in curtailing many of our remarks. Perhaps it would be impossible to write on a subject on which less assistance could be got from other writers, and we have therefore been thrown back on our own observations through life in our own native place for what has been given. There may be persons who have seen some matters in a different light to us, as the same events and occurrences do not always make the same impressions on all. Others may think we ought to have noticed some features omitted; and probably this is true. But had such persons written and noticed those neglected matters, it is just possible that we have mentioned others which they might have left out. However this may be, if the young people be anything like what we were at their age, they will have felt interested in knowing what their grandfathers and some of their great-grandfathers were thinking and doing whilst moving about in Pudsey. We have often spent hours in telling our children about old-time notions and customs in village life. They hardly ever tired of listening, and often asked for more; and it is reasonable to conclude that other young folks will have a similar curiosity.

PLUG RIOTS

We have just received a letter from a Pudsey friend of ours*, saying that we had "hopped over the Plug Riots." Our apology is, that we are aware of having "hopped over" many things, but having so many matters bearing more directly on Progress in Pudsey, we passed them by. We might have noticed several severe panics experienced, the visit of Asiatic cholera in 1832, the passing of the first Reform Bill, the foolish strike at the Waterloo Mill, and the terrible suffering of many families consequent thereon, our own included; the Factory Act in 1834, the agitation against the old Corn Laws, their abolition, and the great pudding in Pudsey at the celebration; the old practice of blood-letting, or bleeding and leeching people to weakness and death, taking away blood from such as needed more, as the doctors now would say; the more recent pulling down of the old church in Chapeltown, etc. But to have done so would not have been strictly within the limits marked out for ourselves; we did not mean to write a mere narrative of events and occurrences, though many more than the above have been before our mind whilst penning our various sketches of progress.

As to the Plug Riots, thereon hangs what might be made an important tale, varying in the minds of lookers-on as they might happen to view their causes and results. Those Riots did not originate in Pudsey, but were perpetrated by outside invaders, though some Pudsey people did get mixed up in the affair. Some years ago, with no intention of ever printing it, we wrote our own Biography or Reminiscences for the sole gratification of ourselves and family, containing twice as much matter as our present Letters on progress, from which it may not be out of place to give a brief extract, which we should not have done had we not received our friend's letter referred to above. The following was written in our manuscript: "The summer of 1842 was one long remembered by hundreds of thousands. Trades of every kind were deeply depressed, and it appeared as if most of the labouring class would be starved to death." Then follows an extract from the "Annals of Leeds" where Mayhall says: "A fourth part of the population of Carlisle were dying of famine. In Stockport, half of all the master cotton spinners had failed, and five thousand working men were walking the streets in distress. In

*Mr. Simeon Rayner, who died very suddenly a few weeks after.

Lancashire the distress was enormous, and was aggravated by a
general turn-out in several branches of trade. In the principal
towns of the West Riding the working classes endured many pri-
vations. At Leeds the pauper stoneheap amounted to 150,000 tons,
and the guardians offered the paupers 6s. per week for doing
nothing, rather than 7s. 6d. for breaking stones, and the poor
rate had increased 50 per cent, and the misery of the working
class made them turbulent." Our own remarks are then continued as follows: "I saw the plug drawers at Bankhouse and
Fulneck, etc. The rioters marched there led by a man of the
name of North, who lived in the neighbourhood of Bradford and
was well known since that time in the same locality as a political
reformer. When the magistrates appeared at Bankhouse accom-
panied by the military—the mounted Lancers—and read the
"Riot Act," this man North stood up and addressed them, telling
them that all his men had resolved to shed no blood except in
self-defence, but had determined that no more work should be
done till the "People's Charter" was the law of the land. He
bared his breast as he spoke, and told both magistrates and sol-
diers, they might pierce his heart with bullets or lances, but the
people were resolved to no longer starve when there was an
abundance in the land, kept from the producers of all wealth
by bad and unjust laws. The magistrates then left, guarded by
the military, whilst scores of stones and broken bricks were
thrown at them over some cottage houses in Bankhouse Lane,
where the road was much lower than the houses. The Bankhouse
Mill boiler was plugged, and the Fulneck Bread Bakery emptied,
as well as many other houses, to supply the hungry invaders.
Much valuable property was destroyed, and scores of Mill boilers
in various places were plugged, and many mill dams let off. I saw
North stand on an iron pipe in Claughton Garth Mill dam, and
heard him tell his followers not to let it off, for in a few days
they expected getting all they wanted, and to let off the dam
would prevent the people from working for a long time to come.
North at that day was a fine looking person, had a good address,
was bold and self-possessed, had a clear and distinct expression,
was very fluent in speech, and just the man to fill his followers
with confidence. These Plug Riots were not confined to one place,
but occurred at the same time in many of the manufacturing
districts in Lancashire and Yorkshire, etc., led by various leaders.
I had always been a Chartist since I knew what politics meant,
and was one then, but not in favour of physical force, and took
no part in any riots. After the sad scenes of that day, I wended
my way home across the fields from Bankhouse, full of solemn
thoughts about the sad and terrible state of the country, and

being but a young man (though married at the time) and not
having much experience of riots, from all I could hear and see
it seemed to me that order and quiet would never be restored
till the Government was changed to a pure Democracy. In this
I was mistaken. Many of the ring-leaders were sent to prison,
while some I was personally acquainted with embarked for
America to escape, and North managed to evade the vigilance
of the authorities by sailing to that country. Matters soon began
to move on as before, the bulk of the people being on the verge
of starvation, while many were starved outright. Though opposed to riots, I could not help sympathising with the object the
rioters aimed at, knowing that the turbulence was the result
of unjust and class legislation, and that it was the rulers of
England who were in reality to blame for the Plug Riots. The
masses of the people had no more political power at that time
than the negro slaves, and therefore could not feel the responsibility that true citizenship gives, for when a people feel themselves aliens, by being excluded from the social compact, they
are apt to attribute to misgovernment more than may really
belong to it, and hence the dissatisfaction and riots, which are
the natural results. Whereas when the people have equal political
rights, and anything goes wrong in legislation, they naturally
look to themselves instead of the rulers for the remedy, and elect
such men to represent them in Parliament as will correct the
evils from which they suffer. So that political power serves as a
schoolmaster, self-reformer, and restrainer of reckless, violent,
and lawless conduct.

As to the various agencies which have effected progress and
produced so much change in the lives and habits, as well as the
general appearance of Pudsey, we have already in our various
articles mentioned some, and will only state here that they have
been two kinds, Voluntary efforts, and Legislative enactments:
the Mechanics' Institute, Temperance Society, Bands of Hope,
Co-operative and Building Societies, etc., while the rural police
have done much to check and destroy the once disturbing ele-
ments of roughness and rudeness in the streets. A good law tends
to restrain bad conduct, and to change public opinion, while an
enlightened and healthy public opinion enacts good laws; so that
law and public opinion act and re-act on each other. The power
given to Local Boards by Parliament has helped to cultivate a
better taste in building dwellings, secured better drainage, and
effected many other sanitary reforms. The once barbarous custom
of bull-baiting was put down by law, but after it was made illegal
the taste and desire for it gradually died out, and that cruel and
degrading sport produced in the minds of after generations both

wonder and disgust. The same remarks would apply to many
other habits and customs, such as the once prevalent pugilism,
dog and cock fighting, and cruelty to animals generally, and above
all, more recently by our national and compulsory system of education are the future generations being improved. We must not
forget in addition all our newspapers, and the general diffusion
of knowledge thereby. Perhaps the greatest reform of all by legislation is yet to come. We refer to the present system of licensing
the public drinkshops before mentioned. The people are certain
before long to demand that every locality shall have the power
to object to them being placed in their midst against the wishes
of the inhabitants residing there.

Therefore it will be seen that the various agencies at work in
effecting the change and improvement in Pudsey, have been both
local and general—by efforts made by the people themselves, and
also by those means in which the whole country more or less
has shared along with the Pudsey people.

OUR CRITICS

We do not claim perfection in what we have written, but are
aware of many defects in style, and to some extent of having
repeated ourself, which is difficult to avoid altogether in dealing
with a subject like this, there being so many matters insepar-
ably connected, and interweaving themselves into each other.
But during the thirty-five weeks our Letters have appeared in the
Advertiser many letters have been sent thanking us for the true
and faithful pictures given of Pudsey and its inhabitants in
times long since passed away. Some of them have been too flat-
tering to publish, to have done so would have been egotistical.
Many, as already hinted, have expressed a desire that what we
have written should appear in a separate form, giving their
reasons for this. There are all kinds of persons in the world,
and there may be some so hypercritical as to find fault. He would
be a most wonderful man who could have written on this subject
and pleased and satisfied everyone. However, both the verbal
and written criticisms we have heard and seen have all been
friendly and favourable except just one, sent on a postcard,
bearing the Wortley postmark, but without the writer's name,
and respecting which a promise was made in the *Advertiser* at
the time that it would be noticed in our concluding Letter. After
thinking over the matter since—and considering that the writer
was afraid of anyone knowing his name—had no promise been
made, we should not have deemed it worthy of notice. As it is,
we will make a few observations, after inserting all the said postal
contains, which is as follows:—

"What rot you write about Fulneck! There is nothing whatever of the communistic principle about the inhabitants; the males and females do not live apart, but a few old ladies do lodge in a house by themselves. No men live separately, nor have they done for thirty-six years or more. You would not have boys and girls board under the same roof, surely. They certainly sit separately in Chapel, so do the Roman Catholics and all German Churches as well. Go and make inquiry before you write such nonsense. ONE OF THEM."

If the above was written by a Moravian, as the writer claims by signing himself "One of them," we are sorry for it, as we had been led to believe better things of the "United Brethren," and did not expect any of them would have written such remarks on what we had said on Fulneck; for always having a good opinion of the people there, we wrote nothing we considered in the least derogatory to their character, but what on the contrary would meet with their approval. The writer cannot have understood what we wrote on Fulneck; otherwise he would have known that most of what we said referred to that settlement long before the last thirty-six years, and to a time when we were well acquainted with it, and from anything we know to the contrary, to a time when the writer of said postal was unborn. The writer says the males and females do not live apart. Does he mean there are no Sisters' and Brethren's parts on each side of the Chapel, which we said? He asks if we would have boys and girls all live under the same roof. We never said we would, and never complained of their separation. It is a wonder this writer acknowledges that the sexes sit separately in Chapel, but as if half ashamed of it, he gives some excuses, saying the Catholics and Germans do so too, whereas he had no need as we never complained of the practice, or thought it wrong; we were simply stating facts. In our Letter on Fulneck we said there was "much of the communistic principle in operation there," but did not use that term in any way objectionable to any intelligent member of that community, but rather of admiration on that account, as any reader of our last Letter on Progress in the Future may see from our views and sentiments expressed there. Possibly there is less of the communistic principle in operation at Fulneck than formerly, as most communities change with time. There may be less exclusive dealing in trade, and more intercourse with the outside world. It is possible that what we read in the "Encyclopaedia Britannica," though written by a clergyman of the "United Brethren" seventy years ago, may not all of it be strictly true today. Amongst many other things it is there stated that before the Sacrament each communicant must converse with one of the elders on the state of his soul. That Lovefeasts were frequent, and on Maunday Thursday (the day before Good Friday), the society had a solemn footwashing, that is, washing each other's feet. Edward Baines in his Directory says, writing on Fulneck: "There is a house for single brothers, and another for single sisters, and a third for widows. These," he adds, "with the houses for separate families, form a considerable village, and various branches of trade are carried on, by which the little colony is supplied with many of the articles of its consumption." And he continues, "This amiable and religious community under a discipline peculiar to themselves, lead a kind of monastic life, compatible however with marriage, and the exercise of trade." From the above quotations and from what everyone else says who knew Fulneck at the time we were speaking of, and even taking Fulneck as it is today, it will be seen that all we said in our remarks on that place and its inhabitants is strictly correct, and that it is not we, but the writer who calls himself "One of them" who ought to go there and inquire before he *writes such nonsense.*"

We have only to add in conclusion, that should it be found that some blunders have been made, we shall be glad to be set right, both for the sake of our readers, and being informed ourself; but thoughtful persons will be most ready to overlook any small errors that may have been made in going over so much ground. Further, and finally: Let it not be thought that Pudsey is all it ought to be. Notwithstanding the great progress made there during the last fifty or sixty years, we by no means think that it has been so great as it ought and might have been. The woollen manufacturers have been too much wedded to the notions of their forefathers, and have not had that spirited enterprise they should have had. They have been too slow to change with the changed tastes and demands of the times, and not only neglected to discover and originate something new, but slow even to lay hold of discoveries made ready to their hands by others, and hence, when at last they have been compelled to change their course, and begin to make a fresh class of goods, it has been after others more wide awake had got the cream in the shape of profits, and left them only the dregs or skimmed milk. Probably in no other locality has so much woollen cloth been made for so little profit as in Pudsey. And if anything we have written should stimulate young people to keep their eyes open, so as to keep up with the general march of progress, and to originate new methods, and thus secure the prosperity of our native place—in which we have spent more than forty years of our life—our labour will not have been in vain.

THE END